NEVER BE
CLOSING

NEVER BE CLOSING

How to Sell Better Without Screwing Your Clients, Your Colleagues, or Yourself

TIM HURSON

AND TIM DUNNE

PENGUIN / PORTFOLIO

PORTFOLIO / PENGUIN
Published by the Penguin Group
Penguin Group (USA) LLC
375 Hudson Street
New York, New York 10014

USA | Canada | UK | Ireland | Australia | New Zealand | India | South Africa | China
penguin.com
A Penguin Random House Company

First published by Portfolio / Penguin, a member of Penguin Group (USA) LLC, 2014

LIBRARY OF CONGRESS CATALOGING-IN-PUBLICATION DATA

Hurson, Tim.
Never be closing : how to sell better without screwing your clients, your colleagues, or yourself / Tim Hurson and
Tim Dunne.
pages cm
Includes index.
ISBN 978-1-59184-676-5
1. Selling.   2. Thought and thinking.   I. Dunne, Timothy, 1965–   II. Title.
HF5438.25.H86767 2014
658.85—dc23
2014004251

Printed in the United States of America
1   3   5   7   9   10   8   6   4   2

Set in Janson MT Std
Designed by Alissa Rose Theodor

To Sid Parnes
mentor, model, friend
Sid, cofounder of the Creative Education Foundation, was
the most persuasive "accidental" salesman we have ever known.

CONTENTS

PART I

Guiding Principles

CHAPTER 1

A Stranger Comes to Town—Why We Sell

All literature is one of two stories: a man goes on a journey or a stranger comes to town.

—Leo Tolstoy

Imagine how life must have been for early humans. They lived in close family groups, probably quite small in size. Because everyone knew everyone else, people wouldn't have much need for selling skills. Within a community, property was likely shared. Exchanging use of this or that item was easy and clear. You knew your neighbor's character, skills, strengths and weaknesses, likes and dislikes, and needs—which were pretty much the same as yours.

Nobody really had to "sell" anything to anyone else.

But then something new happened. One day, a stranger came to town. Your family's first reaction might have been to drive him off, maybe even kill him. After all, who knew what ills an outsider might bring?

But the stranger had something you had never seen before, something to trade—perhaps a tool, a trinket, a particularly well-crafted hunting stick. Suddenly the dynamic changed. You realized there might, after all, be a reason to welcome the stranger, albeit warily.

It's not unlikely that that's how the first sales scenario unfolded.

Of course, the stranger would have had to convince you of several things:

First, that his hunting sticks would be good for you in some way, that they would do what he indicated they would do, that he could be relied on to tell the truth. Ideally, he would demonstrate that he and his "products" were useful.

Second, that his offer was worth whatever he wanted in return. If the stranger wanted that hand ax you had worked so hard to make, he would have had to propose a trade you would see as advantageous.

If your brother or your neighbor needed to persuade you of something, he would rely on his reputation. But the stranger doesn't have the advantage of reputation or status. He would have to find a way to sell you on his proposition.

Not much has changed since our imagined stranger came to town and offered to trade his hunting sticks for your hand ax.

If you sell, and if you aim to sell better, you need to know about the stranger's dilemma.

A stranger doesn't have the leverage of instant credibility. So it's not surprising that a wide range of sales tactics, tools, and closing techniques have been developed as a substitute for credibility. Their purpose is often to wrangle out a commitment to buy, even when buying may not be in the best interests of the client.

The Productive Selling approach we advocate in this book and the courses we teach are designed to overcome the stranger's dilemma, but in a very different way. Productive Selling isn't just a catalog of techniques to wrestle money out of a client's pocket. It's a comprehensive strategy that starts with a well-researched process for identifying and solving problems. In our story of prehistoric sticks and stones, the fundamental reason you and the stranger were able to make an exchange was that each of you solved a problem for the other—you saw value in the stranger's hunting sticks, and he saw value in your hand ax. At its essence, Productive Selling is about helping people solve problems. It focuses the power of a deliberate problem-solving process to help people. It shows you how to access your creativity to establish and maintain relationships that will be truly useful for both you and your clients over time. In a very real sense, this book will show you how to become less of a stranger to your clients. So you can sell better.

———————

Before we start, it's important to make note of the other side of Tolstoy's observation—the second basic story in literature is that a person goes on a journey.

Tolstoy could have simplified his analysis even more: "a stranger comes to town" and "a person goes on a journey" are really the same story—just told from different points of view.

If every client sees the salesperson as the stranger who may or may not be worthy of trust, then every person who sells is that same stranger on a journey—having to prove himself to new people, in new places, with new challenges.

So welcome, stranger. This book is about—and for—you. It's our privilege to take you on a rewarding journey, one that we hope will open your eyes to a new and better way of selling, and that will benefit both you and those you encounter along the way.

CHAPTER 2

Think About It—Think Better to Sell Better

Creative thinking may simply mean the realization that there's no particular virtue in doing things the way they have always been done.

—Rudolph Flesch

Some years ago, we ran an innovation program for the executive team of a large printing firm. The next week, we debriefed with the CEO, a man named Bert. He'd been a semipro fullback before getting into business, and his leadership style was still to run straight up the middle. Bert said, "That was the best sales training I've ever seen. My sales guys need that."

Bert's communication style was so direct that it was sometimes hard to tell if he was being serious. "You want your salespeople to take our innovation program?"

"Nah, they wouldn't sit still for it. But it's the way you guys think. The problem-solving part. They could use that. It's good. Put something together. Short."

The conversation clicked over to Bert's need to plan for his board meeting. In five minutes the meeting was over. That was Bert.

Later, in our own debrief, we started thinking about Bert's reaction to our program. We'd been offering Productive Thinking and creative problem-solving services to organizations large and small, at home and abroad, for much of our working lives. We'd applied the process successfully to innovation projects, strategic initiatives, new product development, marketing, conflict resolution, and even political campaigns. Productive Thinking was so much a part of us that we naturally applied it to our own sales efforts, but it never occurred to us to tailor it specifically to the sales process and offer it to our customers. Bert had seen the relationship in an instant.

And he was right. Fundamentally, the best salespeople help clients solve problems. That's what Productive Thinking is all about. The only difference is the type of problem the client is facing. In Productive Thinking we focus primarily on helping clients with marketing innovations, new product development, process improvements, and so on. Outstanding salespeople solve their own unique set of problems, from cost constraints to supply chain inefficiencies to tight delivery deadlines. But the basic situation is the same: if salespeople can help their clients better understand the challenges they face and offer useful, creative ideas to address those challenges, they are doing their job.

Thanks, Bert.

This book, and the work it's based on, is a result of that simple insight. We know that by using Productive Thinking tools to think about yourself, your client, and the way you interact with each other, you'll be able to sell more—and more effectively—than ever before.

In this book you won't find information about cold calling or qualifying or closing new clients. You won't find the top ten techniques to overcome client objections. And you won't catch us lecturing you about how your main job is to get your clients to make a buying decision.

What you *will* find is a set of easy-to-apply principles and tools designed to help you discover and deliver real value to prospective clients—and transform them into ongoing, productive relationships. Our premise is that selling is not about the art of persuasion. Instead, the best kind of selling emerges naturally from your genuine interest in the person you're working with and your sincere desire to be of use.

Does that sound naïve? Cast your mind back to the last time you felt you were being "sold"—the last time someone employed disingenuous flattery or transparent repetition or obvious closing techniques, like the drop close, the reflex question close, the inverted tie-down, or the ever popular porcupine.* Did you know the salesperson was trying to manipulate you?

---

*We know you probably don't know what these terms mean. We didn't either. But they're great names, even if they describe the kinds of sleazy approaches that give sales and salespeople a bad name. If you want to have a little fun, Google them, and learn how you too can pour snake oil over your customers.

How did it make you feel? Even if you eventually agreed to buy, what are the odds you'll want to do business with that person again?

Productive Selling takes a different approach. It focuses on the long-term relationship you can build with your client and the practical basis for that relationship—your genuine desire to offer value. You'll notice us talking about delivering value and being useful a lot in this book. We think it's a great principle to live and work by. In fact, *Never Be Closing* may be the first sales book you'll actually want your clients to read.

Since Productive Selling is based on our Productive Thinking model, let's start at the beginning—with a brief description of what Productive Thinking is all about, and how practicing its key principles can help you sell better.

As we described in our first book, *Think Better,* Productive Thinking is a structured way of approaching problems and opportunities. Using the Productive Thinking framework, innovators do three essential things:

- Get a clear and accurate understanding of the issues that need to be resolved.
- Define the specific questions that need to be answered in order to resolve those issues.
- Find creative and useful solutions, and refine them so they can be acted on.

In Productive Thinking we break these activities down further into six process steps:

1. **What's Going On?** Rigorously explore the current situation, identify the specific discomforts that need to be resolved, and establish a vision for the future. By doing this, you create a useful context for your further thinking.
2. **What's Success?** Define clear and measurable criteria for success in order to measure the potential effectiveness of proposed solutions. This creates what we call Future Pull—a vision of a future so compelling that it drives you forward, even through the inevitably difficult work to follow.

3. **What's the Question?** Articulate specific questions that need to be answered to resolve the discomfort. Once you find these questions they become catalysts to new ways of seeing your issue and new approaches for addressing it.

4. **Generate Answers.** Suggest creative ideas for answering those questions. The result of this brainstorming will be several solution alternatives. These are not yet full-fledged solutions, but possible approaches to explore.

5. **Forge the Solution.** Refine the most promising answers into robust solutions. This step selects the most promising ideas and forges them into robust, actionable solutions.

6. **Align Resources.** Identify and recruit the resources required to create and execute a plan of action.

In diagrammatic form, the Productive Thinking framework looks like this:

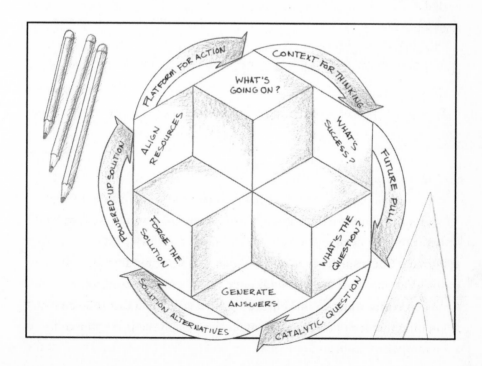

Each step has a set of tools to help people work through the process efficiently, effectively, and creatively.

Productive Thinking is also built on a set of underlying principles— ways of thinking that pervade the creative problem-solving process. They're what Bert was talking about when he said, "It's the way you guys think."

1. Be Aware of Patterned Thinking

The first principle is the recognition that, as creative as we'd all like to think we are, we are impeded by a set of natural barriers that all of us share. We tend to think in patterns. Once we've learned a particular way of doing or seeing something, we tend to keep doing and seeing things that way—often in the face of overwhelming evidence that it might be useful to change. You might recognize these sorts of patterns in yourself—that you sit in the same seat at your breakfast table each day, that you take the same route to work each day, that you use the same words and expressions over and over. You're not alone. We all do it.

This patterned thinking doesn't cause us too many problems when it comes to putting away the dishes or brushing our teeth, but sometimes following our patterns without thinking can get us into trouble. It can blind us to new perspectives and insights. It can cause us to default to "same old, same old" answers when new answers might be more useful.

The Elephant's Tether

The first barrier of patterned thinking is something we call the elephant's tether. Traditional elephant handlers in India prevent elephant calves from wandering by chaining one of the animal's legs to a stake deeply embedded in the ground. The young elephants aren't strong enough to break the chain or dislodge the stake. When they pull against it, the chain tightens and causes them discomfort. Soon enough, they stop trying. As adults, these same elephants can be kept in place with a light rope tied to a stake hammered into the ground with a few strokes. Full-grown elephants can easily break these bonds. But they don't. They become prisoners of a pattern that tells them escape is impossible. For the elephant the pattern of restraint is as powerful as any physical restraint.

Gator Brain

The second barrier is our tendency to defend what we already know and what we already are. We all like to think we think with that big, wrinkly neocortex we see in pictures of the brain, but in reality we do a whole lot of thinking with the more primitive parts of our brains—the limbic system, which produces our emotions, and the stem brain, which reacts instinctively to perceived threats. We call this instinctive part of the brain the Gator Brain.

Science tells us that human beings process just about every experience we encounter first through our Gator Brains, then through our emotional brains, and at the very last through our cognitive, rational brains. That's because the neural fibers that connect our sensory inputs to the three parts of our brains are of slightly different lengths. When your senses pick up a stimulus, the signal travels through your neural network first to the Gator, then to the emotional brain, then to the cognitive brain. All this happens in tiny fractions of a second. It's a matter of biology and physics. And the sequence tells us a lot about the way we react to the world around us.

If you've ever had to slam on your brakes to avoid an accident, you know what we're talking about. First you react: your foot finds the break pedal and pushes hard. Then your emotional brain kicks in and you start to experience fear, anger, or relief. Finally, your cognitive brain kicks in and you start thinking "Wow, that was close!" or "What an idiot!"

That's how we're built.

And it's a good thing. Your Gator Brain has probably saved you from hurting yourself countless times. It's probably even saved your life.

The problem arises when we try to work strategically on a complex task. It's then that our Gator can often get in the way. Think of the last time you were in a meeting and someone came up with a surprising idea. It's almost guaranteed that even before the person finished saying it, your Gator was reacting. And a not-so-little voice inside you was saying, "That's the stupidest idea I've ever heard."

We'll see later in this book how the Gator Brain (either yours or your client's) can ruin a sales meeting. But don't worry, we'll show you how not to become the Gator's breakfast.

2. Separate Your Thinking

The second core Productive Thinking principle—shared by many other problem-solving approaches—is something we call separate your thinking. Here's what it means.

When it comes to solving problems, all of us have two basic modes of thinking. One is what we sometimes call shower thinking—that creative free-for-all style of thinking that many people experience while taking a shower, or driving, or doing repetitive work such as gardening or vacuuming or washing the dishes. It's the kind of thinking that makes all kinds of crazy connections, sometimes resulting in *aha!* moments. We call this kind of thinking creative thinking. It generates ideas.

The other type of thinking is the analytical, rational style of thinking with which we weigh and evaluate our ideas. It's the kind of thinking that measures and compares different ideas to determine which one might be the most suitable in a given situation. We call this critical thinking. It's the judge.

Both kinds of thinking are crucial for solving problems. We need the generative, idea-manufacturing functions of creative thinking, and we need the focused, idea-evaluation functions of critical thinking.

What we *don't* need is both at the same time.

We've all been in a situation where new ideas are put on the table, and the first thing that comes out is a lot of criticism about why the ideas won't work. Less often there's a lot of *positive* feedback about how great the idea is (especially if it's the boss's idea). Both of these judgmental responses—the positive *and* the negative—stop our creative thinking cold. What started out as a brainstorming session ends up being a brain drizzle. Instead of generating lots of possibilities, only the first one or two ever get considered.

What we recommend instead is the practice of separating your thinking. First, come up with lots of ideas without discussing them at all. Have that shower thinking reign supreme, generating one idea after another—good, bad, indifferent, it doesn't matter. Then, after a set period of time or a set number of ideas, go back to that wonderful list and use your rational, critical brain to start evaluating them.

By the simple act of separating the generation of ideas from the judgment of ideas, you end up with a lot more ideas on the table. And, as you'll read further on, the more ideas you generate, the more likely you'll find some that are useful.

Think of it this way. You're a pearl fisher somewhere in the South Pacific. You dive down, pick up an oyster, climb back into your boat, take out your shucking knife, open the oyster, and check it out. Either there's a pearl there or not. You repeat this process for as many times as you can dive that particular day—say, fifty dives.

But what if there's a better way? If you had a pile of sacks, you could take one down on your dive and stuff it full of oysters, then surface, toss it into your boat, grab another bag, and dive again. If you did that, you'd have fifty *bags full of oysters* at the end of your day. Wouldn't that increase your chances of finding pearls?

Most salespeople get this concept immediately. All things being equal, a salesperson who visits one new client a week is going to make a lot fewer sales than the one who visits seven. It's simple mathematics and probability.

Whether it's ideas or sales leads, the more you generate, the better your chance of finding good ones.

3. Reach for the Third Third

The third underlying principle is the concept of the third third. Studies have shown that in great creative ideation sessions, the *first* third of the session produces ideas that tend to be ordinary, run-of-the-mill concepts that most of the group has probably already encountered before. The *second* third of the session is where people start stretching a bit, simply because they've run out of those familiar ideas. And the *third* third is where they begin to generate ideas that are truly innovative and that may hold real promise. In almost all the creative problem-solving sessions we run, it's in that third third that the most promising ideas are usually generated. Unfortunately, most people stop before they ever get to the third third. Often an idea will come up—not particularly new or original or even effective—that *kind of* addresses the problem, so people stop generating new ideas, satisfied that they've reached their creative limit. But is the first right idea necessarily the best idea? What about the second right idea, the third right idea, the hundredth right idea?

Imagine you're hiring for your sales department. Would you flip through a pile of résumés, hire the first person who met your criteria, and then throw the rest of the résumés away? What if there was an all-star hiding in that pile? You'd have thrown away the potential for major success.

So the principle of the third third is don't take the first right answer. Wait till you've been able to generate lots of answers and then decide which one might be the most useful. You'll see how the discipline of waiting for the third third is one of the keys to success in the Productive Selling process.

4. Look for Unexpected Connections

About twenty-five hundred years ago, Heraclitus, one of the earliest Greek philosophers, wrote, "The unexpected connection is more powerful than one that is obvious." Each one of the preceding principles is aimed at helping people find unexpected connections, which lie at the very heart of the Productive Thinking process. By breaking away from patterned thinking, by separating creative and critical thinking, and by waiting for the third third, the chances of finding unexpected connections are dramatically multiplied.

Seeing old things in new ways is what the *aha!* moment of creativity is all about. Archimedes, Edison, and Einstein all opened themselves to the power of these unexpected connections to create their discoveries. And the same applies to productive salespeople. By asking questions and listening with an open mind, they are able to see connections between things, people, and ideas that can produce new and insightful ways to benefit their clients. The art of finding and articulating useful unexpected connections is central to Productive Selling.

5. The Power of the Debrief

Finally, Productive Thinking relies on the principle of the debrief. By applying Productive Thinking tools, you can pull apart, analyze, and reassemble any process. Productive Thinking debriefing tools offer you a self-analyzing and self-learning system, through which you can consistently identify and address areas for improvement. Using these tools, Productive Selling can help you figure out where your sales approach is working, where it needs improvement, and how to make it—and you—better.

Although we hope to give you some very useful starting points in this book, we also believe that the best place to learn a sales process that works for you is in your own backyard. Productive Selling gives you a way to look at your own experiences, extract useful insights from them (both positive and negative), and then apply those lessons to your work as you move forward.

That's the power of the debrief.

Born to Sell?

Perhaps the overriding parallel between thinking and selling is that many people think success in both these activities is primarily a function of natural talent—that good thinkers are simply blessed with good brains, and that good salespeople were just born to sell. There's some truth to both those assertions. Yes, people do have varying levels of creative intelligence, which helps them think more creatively, just as some people have varying levels of social and emotional intelligence, which may help them sell better.

But raw talent is only part of the equation. By applying a set of straightforward tools and techniques, by practicing, and by paying attention to feedback, *anyone can learn to sell better.* In other words, by taking a structured approach to selling, you can leverage whatever natural talent you have and multiply the quality of your output—just as a naturally gifted athlete gets better by learning new skills, practicing them, and adjusting to game situations.

And that's as true for the experienced professional as it is for the novice. No matter how good you are now, you can get better—by acquiring new skills, by practicing, and by extracting meaningful lessons from your experiences.

Our underlying premise is that to be an outstanding salesperson you have to be useful to your client. One of the most effective ways to be useful is to help solve problems. And the best way to do that is to apply Productive Thinking principles and tools to the selling process.

That's why we wrote this book. We want to help you do just that.

CHAPTER 3

Everyone Sells—the Accidental Salesperson

There is nothing in a caterpillar
that tells you it's going to be a butterfly.

—R. Buckminster Fuller

We've written this book for people who sell—people who make their livelihoods by introducing others to the products or services they represent, trying to match those offerings to their clients' needs, and eventually striking a deal that benefits everyone.

We've written it because we think selling is important. Ever since a stranger "sold" his hunting sticks to your distant ancestors, transactions have been the very essence of social systems. People engage in buying and selling—whether products, services, philosophies, or opinions—dozens of times a day. Look around. Everything—yes, everything—made by human beings is the product of thousands of iterations of someone buying and someone selling something.

Although we hope the insights and tools in *Never Be Closing* will be of value to people in sales-related jobs (about one in nine working Americans are employed in sales or sales support roles), this is also a book for the rest of us—those "accidental" salespeople who don't think of themselves as professional sellers: freelancers, consultants, entrepreneurs, and volunteers, whose jobs, community positions, or personal lives involve selling something to somebody almost every day.

The Productive Selling perspectives and tools in the following pages are designed to help anyone who needs to sell, sell better.

- If you're an entrepreneur looking for investors, you have to compete in a busy marketplace to get their attention. You have to get them to say yes to your request for a meeting. You need to identify what's unique and novel about your idea and your plan, and then you have to decide how to communicate your message.
- If you're a small business owner, one of your biggest concerns is developing clients, suppliers, and new partners. You need to demonstrate that you can connect them to resources, tools, and people that can make their businesses sing, and that you can develop a mutually supportive web in which everyone prospers.
- If you're a parent or teacher supporting a new school initiative, you have to get other parents and other teachers to support your proposition. You need to understand what they need, so your proposition has value from their perspective.
- If you're an outside consultant promoting a new organizational strategy for a client, you have to connect with and build trusting relationships with key stakeholders in order to overcome the resistance to change that plagues us all.
- If you're an employee in a large organization angling for the raise you deserve, you'll have to plan when and where to talk to your boss for best effect. You'll have to present yourself in terms that connect with her view of the world, in language that makes sense to her. And perhaps you'll need to review your prior failed attempts, to build on what worked and modify what didn't.
- And of course if you're a professional sales representative for a major supplier trying to close a seven-figure deal, you'll need to show that you know both the risks and the rewards inherent in your client's business, that your offering is right for both their budget and their culture, that you're a valuable resource who can lubricate the path to their objectives, that you do what you say you'll do, and that you'll be around to sort things out if you need to.

The principles and tools of Productive Selling will be useful to just about everyone—because whether we do so reluctantly, accidentally, or deliberately, we are all salespeople.

The Productive Selling process is a structured, practical, repeatable way to help you sell more effectively, and more ethically, than ever before.

Productive Selling leverages the principle that the surest way to earn attention is to pay attention.

Productive Selling breaks the sales process down into discrete steps— steps that you apply based on knowing why you're doing what you're doing. It's a precision navigation system that recognizes that all sales conversations are ongoing transactions—exchanges of value.

Productive Selling starts with the premise that the most important moment in sales is the face-to-face meeting with a potential client. Getting to that critical moment requires careful and efficient planning. Orchestrating that moment requires a specific set of attitudes and skills. And leveraging that moment requires the ability to identify and deliver tangible value to your prospect.

In the end, Productive Selling is about being a better strategist, a better coach, a better business partner, a better colleague. Whether you're a seasoned sales pro, a start-up entrepreneur launching the next big idea, a back room staffer trying to make a difference at work, or a parent looking for effective ways to influence your child, if you're ever in a position of needing to sell anything to anyone, the tools, behaviors, and concepts in this book will help you do it better.

CHAPTER 4

Orion's Belt—
Setting Your Moral Compass

Do the right thing.

—Spike Lee

Since 1976, the Gallup organization has been conducting annual polls about public perceptions of the integrity of people in certain jobs. The findings are remarkably consistent over time. Salespeople don't do too well. One of the reasons for this may have something to do with Orion's Belt.

Orion is one of the largest constellations in the night sky. The three stars of Orion's Belt are among the few formations that can be seen from both the Northern and Southern hemispheres. They are so distinct and easy to find that throughout history they have been as important as Polaris in guiding ships and caravans to their destinations.

Every life benefits from having a North Star or an Orion's Belt to help guide the way. It's easy to lose oneself in the day-to-day pressures of trying to make a living, trying to get ahead, trying to be noticed.

This chapter is about the Orion's Belt of Productive Selling—its three stars: business goals, relationship goals, and intrinsic goals. If you can keep those three stars in balance, you can make the best kinds of sales—those that truly benefit your clients, your organization, and you. But sales is a tricky business, and it can be easy to lose your way. That's why we think Orion's Belt is a better metaphor for us than the North Star.

Polaris is fixed. Its relationship to the earth is always the same. Orion, on the other hand, moves. Its position changes with the seasons. Polaris can be seen only from one hemisphere. Orion can be seen from both. In business and sales, things can change fast, sometimes radically. So it's useful to have a set of values that can keep you on track no matter what the circumstances, the season, or your position on the globe.

Finding your Orion's Belt isn't always easy. But with perseverance and the powerful Five Whys tool, you can locate its three stars and establish a solid platform from which your work will unfold.

I n its 2012 integrity poll, Gallup found that people were most likely to trust nurses, followed closely by pharmacists and medical doctors. At the bottom of the list, the selling professions occupied four of the seven least trustworthy positions. Car salespeople were rated least trustworthy, advertising people were ranked third least trustworthy, stockbrokers fourth least trustworthy, and insurance salespeople seventh least trustworthy.

Whenever you try to sell something, there's a good chance that, consciously or not, your client is tagging you with this stereotype. It compounds the stranger's dilemma: not only are you the stranger, but there's little reason for customers to assume your aims and theirs are aligned. You want something. And your customers assume *they'll* have to pay for it.

Ironically, though, the credibility problem many salespeople face isn't confined to their customers. Their own colleagues and companies may feel equally uneasy about their motives and tactics.

"Don't be silly!" you protest. "My job is to bring in contracts, and that's what I do. As long as I keep performing for the company, they'll love me."

Really? Do you know what your nonsales colleagues say about you behind your back? Have you ever really analyzed the friction between you and the folks in operations, or in customer service, or in finance?

Anyone who's ever sold or supported sales for a complex organization has seen these dysfunctions in action. We know they exist. The question is why.

In 1976 two U.S. economists, Michael Jensen and William Meckling, published a paper entitled "The Theory of the Firm." They argued that businesses suffer when the interests of managers are not aligned with those of shareholders. To rectify this, they proposed that executive compensation be linked to stock prices. As shareholders, executives would, in theory, act in the interests of all the other shareholders of a company. "Shareholder value" became the management mantra heard in boardrooms, in shareholder meetings, and on shop floors across the business world.

Although originally applied only to senior management, this model, known as the Agency model, was soon extended to include other employees. By rewarding behaviors that enhanced shareholder value, even relatively low-level employees could now be "paid for performance."

The Agency model proved to be a jackpot for salespeople. Suddenly, sales commissions and bonuses were no longer seen as simple rewards, but payments that were indelibly tied to business success. They became enshrined in the culture of shareholder value.

All this sounded good in theory. But as one of our favorite philosophers, Yogi Berra, once said, "In theory there's no difference between theory and practice. In practice there is."

It turns out that the Agency model can cause serious problems. It can create a distorted definition of business success, positioning short-term changes in stock prices ahead of quality, employee satisfaction, and customer value. In practice, the Agency model doesn't necessarily do what it tries to do.

It's not difficult for C-suite executives to make a company's book performance look good while at the same time weakening the company as a whole. Liabilities can be buried in off-balance-sheet transactions. Assets can be overstated by selling them to related companies at inflated prices. Books can be adjusted to overstate gains and underreport losses. You don't have to be the smartest guys in the room to paint an overly rosy picture of your company; you just have to want to. Just ask the shareholders and employees of Enron, the suppliers and partners of MCI, or the investors of MF Global.

Even if they have ethical intentions, experience shows that option-incentivized executives are prone to make riskier investments than they otherwise might. Blind adherence to management-by-stock-price proved to be disastrous for scores of companies. A theory designed to create perfect alignment between the interests of management and owners often resulted in practices that did just the opposite.

The same can happen in sales. Few professions are more incentivized to "do the deal" than sales. In theory, paying salespeople to get more business makes perfect sense, but in practice, it's not uncommon for salespeople to benefit more from making the sale than the company does from getting the business. What if to get the sale, the salesperson promises delivery schedules or manufacturing specs or penalty clauses that could damage the business? The transaction that looks great on the top line might be disastrous for the bottom line.

If you're in organizational sales, with only a few, but very large, transactions per year, you've probably heard colleagues say, "We need to get that business at any cost." Really? At *any* cost? The cost of compromising product quality? The cost of overstressing operational capabilities? The cost of burning relationships with suppliers or other customers?

Would a salesperson knowingly conduct a transaction that might hurt the firm? In the abstract, probably not. But would a salesperson knowingly conduct a transaction that might hurt the firm if it made him two million dollars? Would a professional athlete take performance-enhancing substances, jeopardizing his team, her health, and their legacy, if the payoff was big enough?

The Game Trap

If we view business as a game, it can be tempting to view the primary goal as getting the best score (money), and that can often translate into giving yourself permission to operate by the rules of the game rather than the rules of life. After all, "It's not personal.* It's just business."

A convenient little phrase. But is it true?

---

*"It's not personal" may be a useful reminder not to let your emotions drive your decisions, but it's a poor excuse to abandon your values.

Isn't business personal for the entrepreneur who's invested five years of his life in a start-up? For the manager who's wrestled a new division into life? For the team leader who's nurtured the growth of the members of her team? For you when your best client signs with a competitive bidder?

In fact, *it's all personal.* Part of the reason we want to win so badly is that it *is* personal. If you ever find yourself saying, "It's not personal, it's just business," you might have fallen into the game trap.

In the end, the business-as-a-game metaphor is often just an excuse for poor behavior. Whenever you hear someone say, "It's not personal," or its sister phrase, "I had no choice," you can be almost certain they've made a choice they're ashamed of.

The most successful people we know place more stock in the rules of life than in the rules of the game. They live by what they believe, in all areas of their lives—work, home, family. Some are wealthy. Some are not. But most are less stressed, happier, healthier, and a lot more fun to be with.

A re we suggesting that there be no tension between different parts of an organization? Not at all. Dynamic tensions in organizations propel growth—and sometimes even greatness. Creative salespeople can push their companies to new heights. They can help discover new markets. They can challenge manufacturing to develop new ways to meet new needs. They can stimulate operations to develop new efficiencies. So yes, the sales team should be part of the tension that forces a company to stretch. The issue is how to manage that tension.

One place to look for balance is within the organizational structure itself. Salespeople can and should rely on the perspectives of colleagues and risk managers and a management team that weighs short-term benefits against long-term strategies. There are also guidelines available in codes of conduct, conflict-of-interest policies, and corporate values.

The best salespeople also have their own process for balancing those tensions. They recognize that, like everything else of significance in their lives, business *is* personal. And that means the code of ethics they apply at work is identical to the code of ethics they apply at home. It's that observable, reliable set of values that makes you admired and trusted by your clients and colleagues, no less than by your family and friends.

Discovering your root values is surprisingly easy: indeed, most of us know some of them already. You can check them out for yourself by applying the Five Whys tool.

- Choose anything you do and ask yourself why you do it.
- Answer that question.
- Then ask why *that* is important to you.
- Answer that question, and ask why *that* is important to you.
- And so on . . .

Ask yourself why you do something—anything—and by the time you get to the fifth *why?* (and often before), you'll arrive at your values. Living by your root values may not always be convenient, but discovering them isn't very difficult.

I n our work with people who generate business, we've seen a remarkable consistency in those who seem to be guided by their own Orion's Belt. They appear to have found practical definitions of their business goals, relationship goals, and intrinsic goals. And they've synchronized their behaviors toward these three goals with their root values. Most important, they act in accordance with those values in all aspects of their lives.

Here's a distillation of how the most productive salespeople we've met regard their three stars:

1. **Business.** Money is important. It provides me and my family with security, safety, and varying degrees of comfort. Money allows me to invest in things that support my values. But money is not a scorecard.
2. **Relationships.** To the extent possible, I work with people I like and select clients I like. I get genuine pleasure from helping them. As my

relationships deepen, they provide me with increased satisfaction. I recognize that I can neither buy the friendship of others nor sell mine to them. I know I won't necessarily like everyone and everyone won't necessarily like me.

3. **Challenge.** I am energized by puzzles. I get intellectual and emotional satisfaction from understanding and solving complicated and sticky problems. That this makes me money is great but secondary. It bothers me if I am unable to connect with a client or create a solution that works for him or her. Solving other people's problems gives me a buzz and I'll scour the ends of the earth to find an answer.

The three goals above are specific to a large number of salespeople we've met and worked with. There is no right or wrong answer. Most of us are motivated by some combination of material, relationship, and intrinsic goals.

If you know who you are—who you really are—and why you sell, you've discovered your personal Orion's Belt—a never-failing guide to the behaviors that will keep you in integrity. Ultimately your reputation with your clients and your colleagues is built upon those behaviors.

For salespeople, defining a values-based process is clarifying and liberating. Following a process that lines up with your values is one of the surest ways to steer true when the pressure to perform makes decisions seem less clear. The Productive Selling approach and its underlying principles can offer you a platform on which to build your own process that does right by your values, and establishes your own Orion's Belt. We believe that only by being true to yourself can you be true to your clients, your colleagues, and your community.

Everyone knows someone about whom people say something like, "I'd do business with Al anytime, anywhere."

Wouldn't it be great to be Al?

PART II

Setting the Stage

CHAPTER 5

A Simple Story—People or Process?

Study the science of art. Study the art of science.
Everything connects to everything else.

—Leonardo da Vinci

N ow that we've introduced you to our guiding principles, we're going to tell you a story to illustrate some subtle and some not-so-subtle points about selling. We'll build on these points throughout the rest of the book. The story itself is simple—and typical. You may see yourself in it. If so, take note. What follows is fiction, of course. But it's based on hundreds of true stories that we've heard (and, yes, we admit it, experienced) over the years.

S teve Stillman was the head of the market intelligence team at Discus, a fabricating company. Discus was in its second year of a strategic growth initiative. It had brought on new people with world-class skills, expanded its physical plant and capabilities, and was trying to position itself for markets that had previously been too complex for it to service. As the newest junior partner, Steve had agreed to call on selected contacts from his previous jobs to see if he could bring in business. Though he had had some business development experience, Steve didn't think of himself as a true salesman. Still, there was value in getting a feel for the market with face-to-face meetings, and if he could work a previous relationship into a contract, even a small one, his stock would go up with his partners.

One of his first calls was to Ian, with whom he'd worked on a possible joint venture several years before. At the time, Steve was with an investment firm that was looking into new ventures, and Ian's company, Javelin, needed capital to move forward. The two companies never did work out a deal, but Steve had enjoyed working with Ian. He had a feel for him as a person, and he knew the sort of issues his firm faced.

Ian started the meeting as soon as they sat down. "There are several companies like yours who give me great service. Why should I work with you?"

Though Steve had expected some friendly small talk before getting down to business, he was ready for the question. Discus brought some significant competitive advantages to the table. He was eager to communicate that, and had rehearsed several short scripts to make his points. His opener went like this:

"The partners in our firm have expertise in the complete life cycle of our product. Brad Haldane is our supply chain specialist. He's built a flexible network with contracts that guarantee we get the best price on materials. Do you remember when Foil reduced their cell phone prices? That was Brad. He was consulting to Foil at the time and showed them how they could knock twelve percent off the cost of their supply chain in twelve months. He's world renowned in his niche. In fact, he's the featured keynoter at the supply chain conference in Hong Kong next month. Because of Brad's network, we've been able to beat or match every quote we've come across so far for the quality of product we deliver. Part of our service is to have Brad on tap to help our clients improve their supply chain."

Ian was friendly, but far from convinced. "I've heard about Brad, and people speak highly of him, but we work with some of the biggest suppliers in the industry. I'm sure they have the same experience as your firm has. Probably more. You guys are growing. But you're still small. And new."

Steve was ready for this too, with his second script. "I can't argue that. But we see small and new as advantages. *Small* means agile, and *new* means state-of-the-art. And remember, we're only new as an entity. Our people have as much experience as anyone in the industry. Our managing partner is a production line specialist. He's designed our line to be state of the art, which gives us incredible flexibility in what we can deliver for our clients. Our line can be retooled overnight. That means short runs are a specialty of ours. In fact, the production line is the main reason I joined with my partners in the firm. Our breadth of knowledge and flexibility pay big and small dividends to our customers all the time. We saved a client just last week on an opportunity we thought we had lost. When the client realized they had a design flaw and had to re-spec the product, their big-boy supplier couldn't make the change quickly enough. That's where we shine. We were able to retool our line overnight to deliver the change, which allowed our customer to meet their commitments. Bottom line: our flexibility saved their bacon, they hit their delivery target, and we got the contract."

"I won't say that's not impressive, but we don't need that level of flexibility. We use the product in a standard way, and our lead time is long. I can't remember ever going out to bid and then having to change our specs after. Though I agree it would be a nightmare."

"It was. Or it would have been if we hadn't been on the case. It was the first time they ever had to change their specs too. You never know what can happen."

"Well, I can't speak for your other client, Steve. But my bigger concern is about scale. You have one production facility. What if it goes down?"

Steve took this as an opening. "You should come see our facility. I'm not exaggerating when I say state of the art. You've never seen anything like it. No production line west of the Mississippi is faster or more flexible. We're the newest line in the country, with built-in backups and redundancies. In eighteen months, the line hasn't been down more than eight hours, and that was just after we opened. We've never missed a commitment. You won't lose any sleep with us."

"You speak with the same certainty I did about never having to change a design spec." Inside, Steve winced, but he tried not to show it. "Look, Steve, I'm sure you guys have made strides, but I still don't get why you can execute more efficiently than my existing providers. . . ."

"It's exactly what you said before. We're the new kids on the block.

Everyone in our company is intimately involved with every client. When we need to hop, everyone is on board. The only thing we've gotten rid of is bureaucracy." Steve had been hoping to get the bureaucracy line in.

Ian seemed to be warming. "The benefit of small."

"Yes, but not only small. It's also the depth of our management experience. You could say we punch above our weight."

"I'll grant you that."

S teve left the meeting thinking he'd done a pretty good job. He had worked in Brad's Foil story, the upcoming supply chain conference, and the state-of-the-art flexibility of Gary's production line—all compelling stuff, backed up with statistics. He was clear about his team, Discus's suite of products, and their competitive advantage. He identified relevant examples of how they'd helped clients in the past, and linked them to Ian's own situation. His preparation work had paid off.

Steve stopped for a celebratory beer at the station before his train home. As he sat at the bar he added to his mental list of things he was pleased with. "I didn't waste words. I was always on point. Whenever he raised concerns, I answered each one smoothly. I thought well on my feet." He thought there was a good chance he might have brought in some new business for Discus.

Halfway through his beer, Steve's cell phone rang. It was his partner Brad with a question about another project Steve was spearheading. Then Brad asked, "You had your meeting with Javelin today, yes? How did it go?"

"Really good I think. Thanks."

"What did you learn about their supply chain?"

"Well, we focused on other things. They were impressed."

Brad paused a beat, then, "Let's chat tomorrow. You can fill me in on what you learned. Three o'clock?"

S teve enjoyed the cold of his beer, and imagined how the next steps with Javelin would play out. He glanced at his phone for the time and noticed an e-mail from Ian. Good news comes fast, he thought. He opened the e-mail.

Ian Mitchell

To: Steve Stillman
Re: Our meeting

Steve, good to see you today. Thanks for coming by. I had a chat after our meeting with my boss and our purchasing guy, and I wanted to let you know we've decided to stay with our existing suppliers. Best luck with your new organization. Sounds like you have a good core. We can revisit again in 12–18 months.

Ian

Steve cursed to himself, decided not to finish his "celebratory" beer, and made his way to the train platform. He stepped onto the first car, and scanned for a seat. Not many available.

Except, as luck would have it, a back-facing seat (always the last to go) opposite an acquaintance of his, Matt Legere. Steve had coached Matt's youngest son in a community basketball league a few years back, and the two men had become friendly, occasionally bumping into each other on the train to or from the city.

Steve plunked into the seat in front of Matt, who looked up from his newspaper. "Hey, Steve. You're looking a bit tired. Tough day?"

"I had a meeting this afternoon with a possible client. I guess it's distracting me."

"You're a sales guy now?"

"Me, no. But we're a small company so I'm taking some client meetings."

"So you're a sales guy."

"No, it's mostly market intelligence, but I also help out on the client management team."

"So you're a sales guy."

"Okay, okay, I am selling. But I'm not a sales guy." He paused. "Which is I guess why I didn't make the sale."

Matt had heard this before, from dozens of novice salespeople. "Take it from a sales guy: sales guys don't always make the sale either. No big deal, though. I've always said sales isn't about sales."

"That doesn't make sense."

"It does to me. It's part of my sales philosophy. I think it's why I'm good at what I do."

From what Steve had gathered, Matt *was* good at what he did. Apparently very good. "So what's your sales philosophy?"

Matt leaned in, mock-conspiratorially. "I'll tell you mine, if you tell me yours."

"I don't know. I've never thought about it." He laughed. "I didn't even think I was a sales guy."

"Well, you must have prepped for the meeting you just had. What were you trying to accomplish?"

"I thought I'd tap into some old contacts. I called a guy I used to work with. I did some background research with my partners at the office, and then scripted some of the things I thought would be compelling about what we offer. Ian's a logical guy. So I thought if I gave him some logical arguments, he'd give us a shot."

"And?"

Steve explained the key points he made about Brad, the production line, and Discus's flexibility.

"So how did he react?"

"Well, like I said, Ian's a logical guy. He likes to understand causes and consequences. I knew that from working with him before. . . . I thought he'd be impressed. I don't know what happened."

"So what was his reaction to all your logic? What did he actually say?"

"I don't know, he just sort of repeated variations of 'Why should we work with you?'"

"And you answered what?"

"I told you. I thought I was giving him good evidence. Now it seems like he didn't even hear it. He kept asking me how we could be more effective than his current sources. He asked, I answered. I thought I did well until the e-mail. Now I think maybe we were just going around in circles. Or maybe there's some hangover from our previous relationship."

Matt listened to a few beats of the train wheels before replying. "Well, that's always possible. Before I go into any meeting I step back and ask myself about the context of the relationship, who I'm meeting, what's the relationship, why I'm meeting them, why are *they* meeting me? Thinking about the relationship focuses my thinking. It can help me readjust if it feels like we're spinning wheels, which sounds like what happened to you. . . . So what was your past relationship?"

"He had some projects, and we were exploring joint venture possibilities. Turned out it wasn't a great fit. But we enjoyed working together. At least I did."

"So he was selling to you."

"No, I was just looking for investment opportunities."

"From your perspective, yes. But what about his? He has a project. He needs your capital. . . . Don't you think he saw himself as selling you on the deal?"

"I guess. I just hadn't thought of it as a sales relationship."

"At some time or another everybody sells. . . ."

Steve laughed. "Everybody's a sales guy, right?"

"We all are. We have to be." Matt thought for a beat. "So in the past he was trying to sell to you, and now the shoe's on the other foot."

"So I'd better get comfortable in it. Is that what you're saying?"

"Yeah, but more than that. Because you won't be in sales for long if you keep having meetings like this. You know, you did him a favor. You let him disqualify you as someone he needs to talk to."

"Really?"

"Really. Look, if you can't demonstrate you're useful to him, history or not, he's got better things to do than replace suppliers that are already working."

"I never thought I'd sell him just because of a prior relationship. I knew he'd see me, that's all. I think we have a lot to offer. That's useful, isn't it?"

Matt leaned in again. "I think I'm getting a sense of what happened. You had a lot to say, and you said it. But it sounds like you didn't get a lot of what *he* was saying. . . ."

Steve started to reply, but Matt put up a hand. "No, hear me out. You were focused on logic and reason. You said so a couple of times. You said that was based on what you knew about him. But that was in a different setting—where he was trying to persuade you, trying to suss out your needs. This was different. What were *his* needs?"

"Well, security of supply, efficiency, reliability."

"And what did you get from that?"

Steve was blank.

"Here's what I'm saying, Steve. It sounds like you didn't ask. You didn't probe into what was driving him. Was there an itch somewhere? I don't think you know. All you know is, he's okay with his current situation."

Steve took it in, though not happily.

Matt continued, softening his tone a little. "Look, we were talking about sales philosophies before. Here's mine: First, it's all about people. Business is people. Sales is people. Unless you understand people, you'll never understand selling. Second, the only way to really get people is to listen to them. And the best way to do that is to ask questions. The more you learn about their situation, the better you can figure out how to help them. And that's the third thing—and this applies to life, business, everything—it's all about helping people, whether it makes you money or not. For me, that's what selling is all about, helping people. The first word is always people."

Steve let out a long sigh. "Wow. I feel like somebody just let the air out of a big bag—me. But it's good. I feel better. Really. I want to know more."

Matt and Steve continued chatting. As they came to their stop, Matt folded his newspaper and stuffed it into the side pocket of his bag. "Look, Steve, I know the people thing may sound a little Pollyanna. But for me, at least, it's sincere. I get a charge out of it. It's what makes me jump out of bed in the morning. Call me if you like. I'm happy to talk."

———

The next morning Steve sat in the coffee shop near his office, jotting down his takeaways from Matt.

Then he noticed someone peering over his shoulder. It was Jane Anders.

Steve and Jane had completed their MBAs together, and she had been his favorite study group partner. She had a way of breaking things down and seeing the through-line in complex case studies. When it came time for action, Jane was a dynamo: smart, brash, and always game for a challenge.

"Stillman, my favorite entrepreneur."

They exchanged hellos, hugs, and forty-second catch-ups. Jane glanced at his list and asked, "Christmas wishes?"

"It'd be a little early. No, I was just reviewing a client meeting from yesterday."

"You're doing sales now?"

"Not exact—Actually, I guess I am. But not well."

"Reminds me of our study group. Fun times. Need a hand? Or an ear?"

"I could probably use both."

Jane pulled up a chair. "Okay, so what happened in your meeting that was good?"

"It wasn't good. That's why I'm thinking."

· Scan context of relationships before meetings
· How not to disqualify myself
· Ask more than talk
· Philosophy of sales
· Sales as helping
· People People People

"Only failure makes you think? There's always something good." Like all good productive thinkers, Jane started her evaluations by looking at the positives. There would be plenty of time to analyze the negatives later.

Steve went over the highlights of his meeting with Ian—that his performance was solid, that he knew his stuff, had strong data, told relevant anecdotes, and was able to refer to Brad's and Gary's experience.

Jane, who hardly ever conversed without making notes, looked up. "So far, so good. What else was positive about the meeting?"

"Well, the fact that I had it. I wanted to meet with people I knew in my old job who could be clients. I asked, and the guy said yes."

"I sense a *but* coming. . . ."

"But I don't think I used my time with him very well."

"Got it, but first: any more positives?"

"I wish."

"Really, nothing? Would he meet with you again if you asked?"

"Yeah, I think he would, though his e-mail said not for at least twelve months." The memory of Ian's note made him slump back in his chair.

Jane leaned back too. "Ah, so you know the meeting didn't have a great outcome. But he's left the door open for another meeting. Not huge, but still a plus. All right, so play the role of an outsider for a moment. You're observing the meeting as objectively as you can. What would your objections be? What would *I* want you to do differently?"

"That's easy. I really didn't have any strategy. I just thought I'd leverage the relationship and deliver my material, which would be enough to start the ball rolling. We'd have a chat and maybe he'd give me a shot at some business. And it would be as simple as that."

As usual, Jane was taking notes. "I'm writing 'How to establish clear objectives before a meeting.' Does that capture it?"

"Yeah, good, thanks. . . . Also, I didn't learn much. My partner asked me what I learned about their supply chain. I couldn't tell him. Actually, the more I think about it, I didn't find out anything about their current initiatives, or what keeps them up at night." Steve remembered Matt's advice about asking questions to find out how to be helpful. He leaned forward. "In retrospect, not asking was huge."

Jane looked up from her notes. "So 'How to explore for useful information'?"

"Yes, and I didn't really build on our past relationship. There was almost no personal talk. Of course, he didn't help much there. He just launched into questions without any chitchat."

"Okay, so I'll write that as 'How to invite disclosure and make personal connections.' Right, this is a start. No answers yet, but some possibly useful questions."

Steve realized he'd been noticing the words *useful* and *questions* a lot in the last couple of days. "Yes, thanks, very useful." (That word again.)

"No worries. I have to run, but before I do, here's a little script from me. When I asked what was good about your meeting, you used the term 'my performance.' You're right. A sales meeting *is* a performance, but you're not the star of the show. Selling is a process. It's a craft, like cooking. You don't just throw a bunch of ingredients into a pot and expect a gourmet meal. You need the best recipe, the best ingredients, the best tools. You need to add each ingredient at the right time, and in the right way. You need to know what to hold back. You need to preheat the oven. You need technique. After all, your goal is to make the sale. Hear that word *make*? Selling is a craft. The first word is always *process*."

Steve smiled. "That's a good script. And not surprising coming from you."

"I know. You used to call me the process queen. But believe me, it works. I'm doing well—very well. I have a process for before the meeting, for after the meeting, and several for the meeting itself. My process is great . . . for me. If you want my advice, figure out a process that works for you. It'll keep you on track. And most of all, it'll help you sell better. Gotta go. Here's your homework. Or at least some of it. Bye!"

She tore a page from her notebook and slid it to him. Then darted out. Just like at school.

Steve looked at the notes.

Good	Areas for Improvement
· Got the meeting.	· How to establish clear objectives before meeting.
· Knew my stuff.	· How to explore for useful information.
· Delivered relevant information.	
· He'd meet with me again if I asked.	· How to invite disclosure and make a personal connection.

Steve thought about the advice Matt and Jane had given him. Both seemed useful (that word again), but they were coming from very different places. Matt said sales was all about people and that Steve would have been more successful if he'd paid attention to Ian as a person. Jane said sales was all about process, and that he would have been more successful if he'd been like a chef with a recipe. Separately each conversation made perfect sense. Together they were confusing. People or process? Who was right?

CHAPTER 6

Sales Call Forensics—of AARs and BARs

Experience is simply the name we give our mistakes.

—Oscar Wilde

Although Steve got a lot out of his meetings with Matt and Jane, he was still perplexed. Both were successful salespeople, yet they seemed to take very different approaches to their work. Matt was all about people. Jane was all about process. Both seemed to make sense. Whether it was his primary job or not, Steve now appreciated he'd have to become more effective at selling. And that meant figuring out an approach that worked for him.

He needed to speak with Virgil.

Virgil was Virgil Walker, a retired business exec (and lots of other things) who'd mentored Steve through his decision to leave Athelon Finance and take up the junior partnership offer from Discus. Sorting through the issues hadn't been easy. Steve had been with Athelon for six years, he liked his colleagues, and his career track was almost assured. His future with Discus was less clear: the idea of an equity stake was certainly attractive, but the company was new, with all the risks of a start-up—on top of which, he'd be facing a steep learning curve. Throughout it all, his talks with Virgil had been useful. Virgil never gave advice, but had a knack for helping him see things more clearly. In the end, the choice had been straightforward: Athelon offered the comfort of security; Discus offered the discomfort of stretch. Steve had chosen stretch.

Which was exactly what he was feeling as he tapped Virgil's number.

"Can I buy you lunch, Virgil?"

"Sure. Need a talk?" After his retirement, Vigil had started coaching people like Steve who were trying to navigate their careers. He never took money. His view was that his own learning had come with the help of others, and he was more than happy to pay it back. Besides, he enjoyed the interaction. The free lunches were just a bonus.

They met at Virgil's favorite haunt, near the public library where he volunteered. It was an old diner with booths, chrome-trimmed benches, and Formica tables complete with chrome condiment caddies holding salt, pepper, toothpicks, and paper napkins. After a couple of burgers and small talk, Steve gave Virgil a rundown of his sales meeting and what he'd learned from Matt and Jane.

"You were surprised at your friend's observation about the value of disqualifying salespeople, weren't you?"

"Well, surprised at the time, though now it makes perfect sense."

"When you're running an operation, anything you can do to take something off your plate has value. Probably more so now than when I was in the thick of it."

"Yeah, I actually do it myself—though I'd never thought of it that way before. And I certainly never thought of it from the opposite side of the table. I kind of walked into it, didn't I?"

"Well, it sounds like you took a lot for granted."

"I see that now."

"Maybe you should look into the armed services."

"You think I was that bad?"

"Probably. But don't knock it. One thing about the army is that it's a learning organization. But I'm not suggesting you enlist. Just that you learn. You know what an AAR is?"

Steve shook his head. So Virgil began to explain the story of the U.S. Army's OPFOR unit. As part of its training program for its most experienced fighting brigades, the army pits them against an elite unit called OPFOR (short for Opposing Force). In a series of intense simulated combat exercises, OPFOR stretches the trainees to the limit, sharpening their fighting skills and their strategic thinking. As part of the exercise, the brigades-in-training are given better field position, better intelligence, better technology, and twice the manpower. Despite these disadvantages, OPFOR almost always wins the simulations. Why? Because OPFOR debriefs and learns from every engagement. They've perfected the use of a powerful learning dynamic: the After Action Review, or AAR.

Steve was impressed. "You were involved?"

"In a small way. But that's not important. What's important now is to do a thorough AAR on your performance to see where and how you can improve. Make sense?"

Steve reached into his bag for his notes from Matt and Jane. "Absolutely, and we already have a head start."

Virgil scanned the notes. From Matt:

- context of relationships
- how not to disqualify
- ask more than talk
- philosophy of sales
- helping people

And from Jane:

- establish clear objectives
- explore for useful information
- invite disclosure
- personal connections

He looked up at Steve, then put the notes aside. "These are good, yes. And they'll come in handy later. But we're not ready for them yet. First, we need to set a context. Why do you think the AAR is so effective?"

Steve thought for a moment. "Well, it seems obvious. They use it to evaluate their performance. They learn from their mistakes. And from their successes too, I guess."

"Good so far. What do they evaluate their performance against?"

"Against winning?"

"Let's switch metaphors for a minute. You follow football, right?"

Steve nodded.

"And you know how your team did by what?"

"By its won-lost record over the season."

"Right, but does that tell you what makes them a good team? Would their record alone give you enough information to recruit and coach a winning team?"

"Well, no, of course not."

"What else would you need?"

"Well, you'd need to break down the skills in each critical area, figure out how they contributed to the performance, and build from there."

"Exactly. So before the AAR you'd have to set up something to measure against. . . ."

Steve was getting it. "You'd need a Before Action Review to set up your target outcomes and performance criteria."

"Right. Exactly what OPFOR does. Every AAR is measured against a BAR."

Steve was in the flow now. "So you're saying it's not just the score at the end of the game. It's knowing how you got there."

"That and a little more. Just like in a football game or a simulated battle, you'd break it down into step objectives, each one leading to the next."

"Which means we have to define the step objectives for the sales meeting." Steve always got a charge out of his meetings with Virgil. He hadn't ever thought of it this way. He'd assumed that by delivering some compelling scripts, combined with a positive attitude, and maybe a few persuasion techniques, he'd have a decent shot at generating business. He wasn't sure exactly where Virgil was going, or how he'd get there, but he was intrigued.

"Okay," said Steve. "I'm ready. So where do we start?"

Virgil reached into the condiment caddy and pulled out a handful of toothpicks. "With these."

Steve had learned not to be surprised by Virgil's coaching techniques. Virgil fanned the toothpicks across the table. "Have you ever heard of nim?" Steve shook his head. "It's a simple game. You've probably played it. The idea is to start with a number of toothpicks or markers of some kind. You then take turns picking them up according to a set of rules. And the person who picks up the last one wins."

Steve remembered. He had played it a few times at school. In the version he knew, you laid out fifteen toothpicks. You and your opponent took turns picking up one or two toothpicks. The goal is to pick up the last one. Most people figure out that to get the last toothpick (number fifteen) you need to get the twelfth. And to get the twelfth you need to get the ninth, and so on. Once you got the trick, it was easier than tic-tac-toe. If you use the right strategy, you can never lose.

"So using nim as a model, let's play our own version of the game," Virgil continued. He lined up a row of toothpicks so they looked like a picket fence against the white tablecloth. He pointed to the last toothpick in the line. "Let's say this is the final goal of your sales meeting. And the other toothpicks are things on which that final goal is dependent. Each toothpick depends on the toothpick before it. In other words, you can't pick up any toothpick until you've picked up the one before it. Okay?"

"I'm game."

"Good. So what's your final goal? What's the outcome you're after?"

"Of the sales meeting? . . . To make the sale."

"Really? All you want is the sale? What if you didn't make the sale at the end of your meeting, would you consider it a failure?"

"Well, no, not necessarily. Not if I'd made some progress. Maybe planted some seeds." Virgil didn't say anything. Steve sat in silence for a moment, then continued, "I'd want to leave a positive impression. That would be a partial success, I suppose."

"All that work for a good impression? What about those seeds you mentioned?"

Steve couldn't help flashing his frustration. "Okay, so I want to sow the seeds of a scintillating relationship. Is that what you're saying?"

Virgil smiled. "Not bad. Hyperbole can be a useful way to get a new perspective, but how about just a productive relationship?"

Steve refocused. As usual, Virgil was right. "Actually, that's pretty key. Sales on our scale don't happen from a single meeting."

"And . . . ?"

"And it isn't just about one sale either. Ideally, you'd want it to be an ongoing thing. So, yes, a productive relationship."

"And you'd be happy with that?"

"Well, yes. Especially since it's not just about the first sale. There's always the possibility of the second sale and third one and the one after that."

Virgil slid the last toothpick forward toward Steve. "Good. So that's your target future.* A relationship. What's the thing you'd have to do before getting to that goal?"

"Okay, well, I guess you'd have to demonstrate there was a foundation for that relationship."

"And what's the best way in a business context to do that? What do people value in a business relationship?"

"Being trustworthy, keeping your word? Demonstrating you've got something to offer and that you can be relied on. That's how it is for me, anyway. If someone shows me that they can help me achieve some goal of my own, I'll tend to be open to them."

"Right. In my experience, a useful promise kept is the foundation of every productive business relationship—maybe even any relationship. So . . ." He slid the second-to-last toothpick forward. "Make promises that are useful to your client—a big job for a skinny toothpick."

Steve saw where this was leading. "It is, but I get it. Because to make a meaningful promise, I have to have an idea of what would be helpful to them, I have to understand their issues. That means I have to do more asking than talking, which is what Matt said. And Jane too, when she said explore for useful information."

"Good again." Virgil slid another toothpick forward. "And what do you need to do in order to be able to ask useful questions? Keep in mind that those questions might also be challenging to your client."

"Well, in a way they'd have to give you permission to ask certain kinds

---

*In the Productive Thinking methodology, the term *target future* is used to describe a desired outcome.

of probing questions. If you asked them too soon, they might just back off or close down completely."

"Which means?"

"Which means credentials, in a way? I'm getting lost."

"No, you're close. What's the root of the word *credential?*"

"Credible . . . credibility?"

"Exactly. They have to have a certain level of trust in you before they'll be comfortable answering tough questions. So . . . ?"

Steve saw it. "Credibility to get permission to ask questions."

"Bingo. It's one of the most essential parts of your meeting. Without it, you can't move forward." Virgil pushed up the next toothpick. "I call it crossing the credibility threshold."

Virgil and Steve continued their reverse nim. Steve wrote down each step as Virgil pushed the toothpicks forward. Here's what he wrote:

- A successful meeting plants the seeds for a productive relationship.
- To do that, make promises that are useful to your client.
- To do that, explore and ask questions to understand needs.
- To do that, cross the credibility threshold.
- To do that, invite disclosure to find connections with your client.
- To do that, understand who you're talking to.
- To do that, design and manage the meeting dynamics.
- To do that, structure a meaningful agenda.
- To do that, establish desired outcomes.
- To do that, research your client.
- To do that, get a yes to your request for a meeting.
- To do that, understand and articulate who you are and what you offer.

When they finished, Steve leaned back in his chair. "Wow, so that's a BAR. Pretty neat."

Virgil laughed. "No, that's not the BAR. That just gets us to the point where we can do one. The BAR itself is the step where you establish desired outcomes for each meeting—just like the BAR that OPFOR does for each combat simulation. But don't worry about that now. The point is these are the steps you'll have to take before every meeting. Some of them, like your scripts, you'll be able to use over and over. Others you'll probably have to customize for each meeting. And that'll get easier over time. But if you follow this basic approach, your chances of success will increase exponentially.

"Oh, and there's a couple of things I should note at the end that you'll find helpful." He reached across and added a few notes to the end of Steve's list.

Steve looked over the finished list. "So it looks like I've got my work cut out for me."

"That's what excellence is all about. It takes work. That's why OPFOR wins. But look at the bright side. At least now it *is* cut out, instead of in a messy pile."

"True. There *is* something I'm still curious about, though."

"Shoot."

"You just talked a lot about process. You laid out . . ."

"*We* laid out."

"We laid out eleven discrete stages to go through, from scripting to promising. That's pretty process-oriented. Jane said selling was all about process. But you also said that it was critical to understand who you were talking to, connect with them, earn their trust, establish relationships. Those are all people things. Which is what Matt kept pushing."

Virgil waited for the question.

"So if you had a choice, which would you focus on more, people or process? Where's the biggest payback?"

Virgil pushed back his chair and got up. "Which is more important, breathing in or breathing out?" He didn't wait for an answer. "Let's talk again in a couple of weeks and see where you get to. Thanks for the lunch. Next time it's still on you."

T he result of Steve and Virgil's conversation is the chapter outline for the rest of this book—and the essential steps in the Productive Selling model. Here's how it's organized:

- Chapter 7: Select, prepare, and deliver brief scripts about you, your offerings, and the reason for your meeting.
- Chapter 8: Establish enough connection or interest to get a yes to your meeting request.
- Chapter 9: Conduct efficient research for your meeting.
- Chapter 10: Establish target outcomes and success criteria for the meeting.
- Chapter 11: Use a structured template to drive your meeting forward.
- Chapter 12: Understand and leverage the natural dynamics of the sales meeting.
- Chapter 13: Recognize and connect with the thinking preferences of your clients.
- Chapter 14: Use waiting-room time productively and make small talk big.
- Chapter 15: Earn the credibility to ask questions.
- Chapter 16: Ask questions that inform both you and your client.
- Chapter 17: Allow for incubation time.
- Chapter 18: Establish usefulness and plant the seeds for a relationship.

The final four chapters derive from the notes Virgil added to Steve's list.

- Chapter 19: What and how to learn from your meeting experience.
- Chapter 20: Debrief the *process* of your meeting so you can identify areas for improvement.
- Chapter 21: Debrief the *content* of your meeting so you can design follow-ups and contact points.
- Chapter 22: Establish and maintain a position in the headspace of your client as you move forward.

PART III

Preparing for the Meeting

CHAPTER 7

Alfred Hitchcock Presents— the Power of Scripts

To make a great film you need three things—
the script, the script, and the script.

—Alfred Hitchcock

A sales script is a short, rehearsed speech that informs your client about you, your company, your product, or your industry. You can use scripts throughout your meeting—and in many other situations as well. Whether it's on the phone, in a restaurant, or at a conference, a short script about who you are and what you offer can help position you as credible, intriguing, and worth spending time with. In almost any situation, being able to express your essential message quickly and cleanly will set you apart from the crowd.

Scripts are not designed to manipulate your clients, but rather to communicate with them—efficiently, effectively, and professionally. The main purpose of your sales script is to help you establish credibility. As Steve identified in the previous chapter, credibility is what earns you the right to ask questions, and asking questions is how you learn about your clients' issues, perspectives, and needs. A secondary, though still important, purpose is to discover possible personal connections between you and your client. So scripting is essential. Think of it as the first toothpick in your sales process.

Your scripts help you build credibility in two ways: what you say and how you say it. *What* you say is aimed at building your content credibility. *How* you say it is aimed at building your process credibility. Let's start with process.

Process Credibility

Part of establishing your credibility is knowing how and when to deliver information, and doing so in an assured, professional manner. Think about how you react when you meet a professional, whether it's a fitness coach, an investment counselor, a corporate trainer, or a doctor. You respond to the atmosphere these people create. Peter, a young man we know, is a big-city paramedic. He's often told us that although it's his medical and technical know-how that ultimately saves lives, it's his calm, professional manner that emergency patients and their families respond to first. It gives them confidence that they are in good hands.

In much the same way, delivering your first few words with calm confidence signals to your clients that you know what you're doing, and helps them relax.

If you ever attend keynote speeches, you know that you (and most of the rest of the audience) can instantly tell the professional speaker from the novice. The pro steps up to the platform, radiating energy. She shakes the emcee's hand, pauses at the lectern, waits for the room to focus on her, and delivers her opening lines with authority. Before even getting to the heart of her speech, she has the audience's attention and respect. They know that she knows the protocols. They are in good hands. She's established credibility.

Delivering your scripts in a sales meeting achieves the same objective. Often, your ability to follow protocols and speak comfortably about yourself and your company may be enough for a client to relax into the meeting. The battle isn't over. You'll still have to deliver good content, but your style alone can create a platform for your credibility. In order to perfect that style you'll need three things: rehearsal, an audience willing to give you useful feedback, and, of course, practice. We'll talk about all those things later in this chapter.

Content Credibility

The content of your scripts should be informative and relevant. You want to deliver clear, uncluttered information about you, your company, your offerings, and why you think your client will find it useful to meet with you. You also want to be sure the information you deliver is meaningful to your clients. The fact that your company consistently places first in the local corporate fun run may be important to you, but unless your clients sell running shoes it may not mean much to them.

One way to think about your content is to ask yourself, "What will interest my prospective clients enough that they'll want to keep talking to me?" or, "What information can I offer them so they'll feel it was worth their time to meet with me?"

Usually, sales scripts fall into one of two broad categories: background scripts and newscast scripts.

The majority of your scripts will be background scripts that give information about you, your company, your product, or your industry niche. They'll highlight what's unique about you and your offerings. Sometimes they'll take the form of war stories that illustrate how you or your company overcame challenges or constraints and how you went beyond the call of duty to meet your clients' needs. Stories like these are often the stuff of company lore, so a good place to find them is to talk to senior people in your firm. Background scripts tend to be stable. They don't change much over time.

As the name implies, newscast scripts are less about history and more about current affairs. Their content will change over time; for example, how other companies may be mitigating the effects of a new tax ruling or uncertainty around new regulations. Newscast scripts also tend to be less general in nature. They focus on issues and perspectives that relate to individual clients—things that are particularly relevant to them. They may offer your insights about current trends or potential market disruptions. Because newscast scripts often present your interpretation and analysis of changing events, you can use them to differentiate yourself from your competition. A unique and useful perspective on changing business conditions can separate you from the pack, establish you as credible, and provide a springboard to the exploration phase of your sales meeting. You'll see a powerful example of this in chapter 15.

A Menu of Script Possibilities

Scripts are essential. But the idea of designing them can be daunting. Many salespeople shy away from building scripts because they don't know where to start. Page 57 offers some straightforward questions that can provide starting points for hundreds of useful scripts.

These aren't the only places to find potential scripts. Once you start looking for them, you'll begin to see them all around you. Conversations with clients or colleagues are often peppered with raw material that can make useful scripts. The key is to keep your eyes and ears open for possibilities.

How to Build Your Scripts

Back in chapter 2, we wrote about the principle of separating your thinking—first generating lots of ideas and then going back and judging each one. We called it making lists and making choices. This simple principle is the best way to start building your scripts.

Ask yourself any of the questions above or other questions you think might be fruitful, and just start listing your answers. Think about the things you find yourself saying again and again in client meetings, or what you say when you describe your job to a curious friend. Don't worry about whether your statements seem good or bad. Just generate a long list of possible answers. For example, from the table above, you might ask yourself, "What's interesting or unique about me?" Then just start listing. Put your shower thinking cap on and start making random associations, adding to your list of things you've done, things that make you unique, things that seem interesting about you. Anything and everything goes. You're the only one who ever has to see this list. Just keep adding things until you run out of steam—then catch your breath and add some more.

Once you have a long list—and not before—switch gears, and engage

Question	Script	Good for
• What's interesting or unique about me? • Personal anecdotes* can establish you as interesting to know. Stories about your travels, for example, can open conversations about places your clients have visited and may reveal shared experiences and interests.	Background	Connection
• What's my story? • Talking about your professional history can shed light on your experience, expertise, and network of contacts.	Background	Credibility or Connection
• Who's on my team and why are we useful? • Stories that highlight how proud you are of your colleagues and their accomplishments reflect well on both their credibility and yours.	Background	Credibility
• What's my firm's philosophy? • Discussing your company's strategies can give your clients insights into who you are, how you operate, and why you're talking with them.	Background	Credibility
• What's my philosophy about this business? • As above, but from a more personal perspective.	Background	Credibility
• What's happening in our industry? • Scripts that reveal your insights and analytical capabilities can be powerful credibility builders.	Newscast	Credibility
• What's the history of my products or services? • Stories about how your offerings have evolved over time can be springboards to discussions about your clients' experiences and needs.	Background	Credibility
• What's happening at my firm? • Groundbreaking developments or transactions specific to your company can lead to discussions about innovations, markets, and client needs.	Newscast	Credibility
• How have we helped people in the past? • War stories about helping clients identify and overcome their challenges can speak volumes about your capabilities and your approach to business.	Background	Credibility

your critical thinking. Read through your list and highlight the most intriguing, powerful, amusing, insightful, or provocative topics—the ones that interest *you*, and the ones you think might interest your clients.

Now you've got a short list of potential script topics for the first question (*What's interesting or unique about me?*). Go back to the questions above and do

---

*One of us had a script he often used at the beginning of meetings. It was built around a year of global travel that marked a major career transition. The story almost inevitably led to conversations about places clients had visited, and it established Tim as interesting, independent, and unique.

the same for each one. In relatively short order, you'll have a whole library of script possibilities.

Now take a look at all your work and make another selection. Choose the potential scripts you want to build—the ones that might be useful as starter scripts. You might have been developing some of these naturally, as things you tend to come back to in client meetings, because you've received positive reactions to them in the past.

Once you've got your starter list of scripts, you're ready to start writing.

Writing?

Yes. The best way to make sure your script makes sense, says what you want it to say, and is easy for you to deliver is to *write* it. And writing it isn't nearly as hard as you might think.

Creative Writing 101

One reason people panic about writing is that they assume they have to write a final draft on the first go. If you start with that idea, there's a good chance you'll never start at all. The secret to writing is similar to the "make lists, make choices" mantra for generating ideas: you do it a lot better if you separate the job of generating your ideas from the job of judging them. With writing projects, this fundamental Productive Thinking principle is expressed as "First get it down, *then* get it good."

Here's what you do: Start by spilling your guts. You know your subject, at least in part. It wouldn't have made your list if you didn't. Write down everything you know about the issue. Don't worry about structure or sequence or spelling. Just get something—anything—down on paper or in a file. Aim for two to three rambling, sloppy, messy, incoherent paragraphs.

Then read what you've written. From a content point of view, you'll see what's there, and you'll see what's missing. If your first draft seems incomplete, go back to your sources—the people who know the company best and who present it to outside audiences. Talk to your marketing director, your customer service people, your manufacturing experts, your CFO, or other executives. They'll all have ideas of what to say and how to say it. Read your company's marketing material or press releases. There are people in your organization who've done a lot of thinking about telling the company's story. Take advantage of them. If you know people with potentially useful war stories, interview them. Capture both their stories and their language. Then use them to your advantage.

Once you have gathered this material, rework your script. Take out the fluff and put in the beef. It may take a few drafts, but once you have something on paper, it's easier to change or cut than to write from scratch. As you write, keep in mind the seven commandments of a good sales script, listed below.

THE SEVEN COMMANDMENTS OF SCRIPTS

1. Focus on one key point that illustrates something unique or interesting about you or your company.

2. Tell a story. Facts and figures are important, but they're not stories. Stories are about people. Always include people in your scripts.

3. Be relevant. Write general scripts relevant to many clients. Write custom scripts relevant to specific clients.

4. Always finish with a question. Your goal is to learn by asking questions. Ending with a question allows you to check if you've earned enough credibility for your client to answer.

5. Be brief. Write scripts less than sixty seconds in length.

6. Be brief, really. No one wants to be lectured.

7. Always finish with a question. Got it?

Once you have an edited draft, take it for a trial run by delivering it to someone (perhaps your boss or a colleague) who can give you useful feedback. After you've run through it, first ask them what they like about it.* Then ask for their concerns or suggestions. Then rework your copy.

Before and After

Let's look at a few examples of how this process of refining your scripts can turn a good script into a great one.

Here is the "before" version of one of the scripts Steve used during his meeting with Ian:

"The partners in our firm have expertise in the complete life cycle of our product. Brad Haldane is our supply chain specialist. He's built a flexible network with contracts that guarantee we get the best price on materials. Do you remember when Foil reduced their cell phone prices? That was Brad. He was consulting to Foil at the time and showed them how they could knock twelve percent off the cost of their supply chain in twelve months. He's world renowned in his niche. In fact, he's the featured keynoter at the supply chain conference in Hong Kong next month. Because of Brad's network, we've been able to beat or match every quote we've come across so far for the quality of product we deliver. Part of our service is to have Brad on tap to help our clients improve their supply chain."

Here is the same script, reworked based on feedback from Steve's colleagues—and formatted according to our Seven Commandments:

"Remember Foil's ads with the sledgehammer? The sledgehammer that knocked twelve percent off the cost of their product? That twelve percent was due to my partner Brad, who's our supply chain expert. Before he joined us, he consulted to Foil. He tightened their supply chain, which allowed them to pass on massive savings to their customers. Brad was the sledgehammer and now he's with us. Brad thinks about supply chains in a way I've never seen before. His breadth of knowledge stuns me. He's world renowned,

---

*Remember how Jane focused on the positive first when asking Steve to evaluate his meeting? In chapter 20 we'll present a debriefing tool called POWER that takes full advantage of the "praise first" principle.

and speaks at conferences all over. Because of him, we source the best materials at the best prices. Nobody matches our quality at our price. We even offer his expertise to clients, so they can sledgehammer their own supply chains. How do you manage your supply chain?"

Improvements to the script:

- It's more personal—Brad has been personified as a sledgehammer.
- Brad's availability as a resource to clients is overt.
- It's slightly shorter.
- It ends with a question.

Here is the "before" version of the script Steve used with Ian about Discus's production facility.

"Our people have as much experience as anyone in the industry. Our managing partner is a production line specialist. He's designed our line to be state of the art, which gives us incredible flexibility in what we can deliver for our clients. Our line can be retooled overnight. That means short runs are a specialty of ours. In fact, the production line is the main reason I joined with my partners in the firm. Our breadth of knowledge and flexibility pay big and small dividends to our customers all the time. We saved a client just last week on an opportunity we thought we had lost. When the client realized they had a design flaw and had to re-spec the product, their big-boy supplier couldn't make the change quickly enough. That's where we shine. We were able to retool our line overnight to deliver the change, which allowed our customer to meet their commitments. Bottom line: our flexibility saved their bacon, they hit their delivery target, and we got the contract."

Here is the same script after Steve reworked it:

"Our people have as much experience as anyone in the industry. Gary Chang, our managing partner, used to head production at HighBar. He's the main reason I joined Discus. Gary's designed us the best production line in the country. No line is faster. No line is safer. No line is as flexible. We can retool overnight. Just last week, one of our clients realized they had a design flaw and had to re-spec a job. We were able to retool on a dime. From the minute we received the redesign till the minute they received the finished product was less than forty-eight hours. They went from crisis to meeting their commitments. I'd love you to come and visit our plant. You'll see why our clients are so happy with us. Have you ever had a delay because parts couldn't be sourced on schedule?"

Improvements to the script:

- It's more personal—Gary's history and expertise are highlighted.
- It contains some memorable repetition, with the three "No's."
- The anecdote is told from the client's perspective.
- It's shorter.
- It ends with a question.

By using feedback from your trusted colleagues, you can always improve your scripts. There's no doubt that it takes work, but the effort is more than worth it. All that polishing can produce a script as shiny and sleek as a new BMW.

Avoid Traffic Tickets

The problem with a shiny red BMW is that you want to put it through its paces. The problem with having a library of highly polished scripts is that you want to use them. Once you get rolling, it's easy to connect one script to the next and talk too much.

Wall-to-wall monologues are disrespectful, boring, and ineffective. Evil superheroes do monologues. Good salespeople don't.

Remember, the primary purpose of your script is to earn enough credibility for your clients to feel comfortable answering your questions. Give them a chance! Deliver only the scripts you need to, and only *as* you need to, to get to that point.

Once you get into the exploration phase of your meeting (which we'll detail in chapter 16) there will be additional chances for you to deliver scripts, but in the early phases of the meeting, once you've earned the right to ask questions, park that shiny Bimmer in the garage, and get on with the job of discovering your new client's issues, perspectives, and needs.

By the way, this is one of the reasons we say that scripts should always end with a question. It's a way of moving from telling to asking—of putting the brakes on your BMW.

When to Use Scripts

Scripts are most useful in the early parts of your conversation. That's because the primary purpose of scripts is to earn the right to ask questions. But you can also use scripts, as long as you do so judiciously, in other parts of your meeting as well. (You'll find detailed discussions of the meeting structure in chapter 12.)

Using Scripts in the First Part of Your Meeting

Use appropriate scripts early in your meeting (chapter 15) to help get you over the credibility threshold. Delivering a script early can also be a confidence booster. If you've said something useful and said it well, you'll have won a small victory and feel more self-assured as you move on. The content in your script and your demonstration of professional protocol both contribute to your credibility.

Offering a script, especially a personal one, at the beginning of your meeting is also an invitation for your clients to connect with what you've said and share something of their own. Reciprocity is the essence of good conversation. Your willingness to disclose information about yourself and your company invites your clients to reciprocate. After you have spoken for a minute or two, the other person in the conversation will naturally want to say something too. They may want to ask a question, agree or disagree, build on something you've said, or simply affirm their presence in the room. If you talk for a bit, ask a question, and leave space, the other party will almost always enter the conversation. Disclosure invites disclosure.

Using Scripts in the Second Part of Your Meeting

You can also use scripts in the exploration phase of the meeting (chapter 16). The exploration phase consists largely of your asking, and your client answering, questions. Asking questions is essential for you to understand your client's situation, perspectives, and needs, but question after question can also feel like an interrogation. One way to break up what may feel like a cross-examination is to drop in a relevant script. As long as it's short, and ends with a question, this can be a useful way of changing the rhythm and tone of your exploration.

Using Scripts in the Third Part of Your Meeting

The third part of your meeting is where you deliver value to your clients (chapter 18). As you'll read further on, we strongly recommend holding back on delivering this value until the end of the meeting, when it will have the most impact on your clients. This can be an outstanding opportunity to use a prepared script to address specific needs or concerns your client has expressed.

For example, in Steve's meeting with Ian, suppose Ian had said, "We work with some very established companies. We assumed, due to their size, that they would source the best components at the best prices. But we discovered that wasn't true. We did some checking and found there were manufacturers out there who were charging less for the same quality than our suppliers were paying to their traditional sources. Their complacency about their supply chain was costing us money."

Remember the script Steve delivered at the beginning of his meeting about how Brad, the supply chain expert, was able to help another client shave 12 percent off their costs? Imagine how much more impact that information might have had at the *end* of his meeting, *after* Ian had expressed his frustration about pricing. At that point Steve could have delivered real value, and perhaps even opened the door to a followup meeting that would include Brad. Delivered at the beginning of the meeting, the script was a way to build credibility. Delivered at the end, it becomes a way to offer value.

Using Scripts in Other Situations

A script can also serve the purpose of an elevator pitch. You are on the elevator with someone who you've wanted to meet or get a meeting with, and you have thirty-seven seconds to introduce yourself and make a request.

For the same reason, if you are in an industry or situation where cold calling is not equivalent to hanging yourself from the nearest tree, a script can be a useful tool over the phone. Cold calling can be a viable option if there are many potential buyers for your product, or if the opportunity cost of a no to your meeting request is low, or if there are many routes into a client organization. If cold calls make sense in your business, a script is an efficient way to establish your unique proposition. There's a good chance that anyone in a position to become a client will be interested in a quick, clean statement about who you are and what you offer—whether you're at a cocktail party, in an elevator, waiting in line at the movies, or chatting for a moment on the phone. The skill of expressing your ideas crisply, clearly, and in almost any situation is a powerful asset.

A t the beginning of this chapter we quoted Alfred Hitchcock, who believed that the script was the absolute foundation of filmmaking. For him, the notion of a successful film without a script was absurd. We think the same is true for successful sales meetings.

But, like all great strategists, Hitchcock also knew that because reality deviates from the best-laid plans, he had to be flexible enough to adapt to the changing needs and everyday hassles of film production. The same is true in sales. You need to plan, build, and rehearse your scripts carefully, but you also need to understand that it's unlikely you'll use every one of them in a given meeting. Like Hitchcock, you need to stay flexible.

Think of your scripts as building blocks to help you create a strong foundation for your meeting. You can mix and match them as the need arises. You can modify them to fit your client's circumstance and issues. You can deliver them, or you can hold them back.

The point is that simply *having* your scripts in your back pocket will make you more confident, more professional, and more prepared for the unexpected. With a library of well-prepared, well-rehearsed scripts, you'll have a safety line to fall back on if things start going off the rails. Without them, you never know where you'll land.

In a way, all the effort you put into developing, refining, and practicing your scripts is like a concert pianist practicing musical scales: you may not always use them, but you can't play without them.

CHAPTER 8

The First Yes—Get the Meeting

*The victorious strategist only seeks battle
after the victory has been won.*

—Sun Tzu

Ask almost anyone who's ever had to do it, and you'll discover that even the most seasoned salespeople hate the idea of cold calling. Cold calling is the modern-day version of the stranger's dilemma we illustrated in chapter 1. "I don't know you. You don't know me. I have no reason to trust you, and I'm too busy putting food on my table to speak with you anyway."

But what if we could get around the stranger's dilemma? What if we were members of the same community? What if we could find a connection?

Imagine you receive a new set of golf clubs for your birthday. Nice gift. Your old clubs have (mostly) good memories for you, but you really don't need them anymore. You could decide to sell them on eBay or Craigslist. Or you could think about people in your own circle who might want them—maybe a colleague who's interested in learning the game, or the son or daughter of a friend. What do you do? You flip a quick e-mail to your friend, and offer your clubs at a fair price. You wind up with a few extra bucks in your pocket, and your friend's kid gets a good deal on some decent clubs.

You sold your clubs, everyone got something out of the deal, and there was no cold calling involved. Wouldn't it be great if real business could be like that?

Well, it can. And in some ways it's easier than ever.

Unless you plan a career as a robocaller, you need to talk to your prospective clients in order to sell them anything. And talking to people usually means meeting them. So a critical step in the process is getting a yes to your request for that first meeting.

Successful businesspeople are bombarded with requests for their time, often by people they may not know trying to sell them something they may not need. If they're going to stay successful, they have to manage their calendars with care, so it's axiomatic that prospects won't agree to meet with everyone who asks. Your first contact is crucial, because if you do get turned down, you'll have a hard time converting that no into a yes—like asking someone to *un*check an item on a to-do list. Sure, you can keep asking, and persistence has its rewards, but you also risk being perceived as pushy, insensitive, or annoying. Wouldn't it be better to get a yes on your first try? This chapter is about increasing the chances of making that happen.

Referrals from Existing Clients

Far and away, the best way to get a yes to a meeting request is to be referred by one client to another. There are three main benefits of getting a referral:

- A referral gives you almost instant credibility. If Alan Taylor tells a colleague you're worth an hour of his time, not only will you have a good chance of getting your meeting, you'll start it off with a distinct advantage.
- A referral dramatically cuts down on the time and effort you need to spend researching potential client organizations.
- A referral identifies a specific person to meet within your target organization (even if they're not the "right" person, they can usually steer you to the appropriate contact).

The easiest way to get a referral is to ask.

Matt, Steve's "selling is all about people" friend, prides himself on never having to make a cold call. He sees every relationship as an opportunity to develop another one. Matt almost never leaves a client meeting without asking, "Who else might benefit from talking to me?" There's a good chance his contact will have one or more acquaintances who could. Don't think of asking for a recommendation as a selfish act: a good referral can benefit the referrer as much as it benefits you. People generally like to offer other people benefits. Just like telling people about a good book or a good movie or a good restaurant, telling them about a good supplier enhances their own reputation.

If Matt's clients come up with a name or two, Matt goes a step further. He usually asks, "Great, would you be willing to send them an e-mail to let them know I'll be calling? Tell them whatever you're comfortable with— that we've done business together, that you think I might be useful to them—whatever works for you." He then sends his client a simple reminder e-mail.

Matt Legere

To: Ram Sava
Re: Followup and thanks

Ram,
Thanks for the meeting today. I'll follow up with the information on Nordic early next week.

Thanks too for the referral to Pat Silko. Give me a heads-up after you send your e-mail, or even copy me if you're comfortable with that, so I know when to give her a call. Much appreciated.

Talk to you next week.

Matt

Occasionally, a client may balk at offering a referral. Whatever the reason, don't push. Your first obligation is to the relationship you have, not the one you hope to develop. You need to respect your client's sensitivities. We've said several times that we don't believe there are many absolutes in human relations, but here's one: never attack a retreating client. Once you've asked, accept their response and move on.

Not all meetings afford the opportunity to ask for a referral. Perhaps there are others in the meeting, perhaps time is running short, perhaps asking for referrals is a new behavior for you, or perhaps it just doesn't feel right. Whatever the reason, you still have a secondary opportunity. And referrals are so valuable that we suggest you take it. After your meeting, include your request in a followup e-mail like the one below.

> Matt Legere
>
> To: Sylvia Hernandez
> Re: Delivery timings
>
> Hi Sylvia,
> Thanks for meeting with me yesterday. I checked on the delivery timings you asked about, and three days will be a squeeze, but my operations people said they'll pull out all the stops to do it.
> Also, I wonder if you know of anyone else who might benefit from our services. As you know, I found you through Peers Katrin. He was happy to hear that we met. I'd be pleased to call on anyone you know whom I might be able to help.
> I'll get you those delivery quotes next week.
>
> Matt

If you travel in your work, scan your address book for people in cities you'll be visiting to mine for referral possibilities. If you have clients who work, or have connections, in those cities, you can save yourself weeks of searching, strategizing, and stargazing with a straightforward request: "While I'm visiting you in Houston, is there anyone else you can think of who might benefit from talking to me?" or "I'll be making a swing through Southern California in the next few weeks. If you know anyone in the area who might benefit from what I offer, I'd be happy to contact them."

There is no better way to increase your chances of getting a yes to a meeting request than a solid referral. It's one of the biggest gifts a client can give you, but it's one you have to ask for. So be like Matt, and ask for it whenever you can. The more referrals you can get, the more yeses you can get, and the less time you'll have to spend getting them.

Personal Referrals

A referral from a satisfied client is always the most reliable way to increase your chances of getting a yes to your request for a meeting, since it creates a direct connection between someone who's benefited from working with you and your prospective client. But business referrals require a track record. What if you're just starting out in sales, or if, like Steve, you're venturing into a new business sector, and haven't yet built up a robust list of contacts?

The next best connection is a personal one. Any link between you and your prospective client, even if it's not a business link, increases your odds of getting a meeting. To find these connections, you have to do a little research on the person you're trying to meet and then tap into your network.

Steve's business school friend Jane had become a master at finding these kinds of connections. Here's how she explained it to Steve:

"The first thing I do is a Web search to see if the company has an online directory that can help me identify a few key people—product managers or marketing people related to my line of work. If that doesn't work, there's always the phone. I can usually identify relevant people with a few calls to central company numbers. Next step is Googling those names, followed by Facebook and LinkedIn. Even people with fairly common names aren't that hard to research if you know where they work or their professions. Pretty soon I can usually find a Twitter handle if they have one, and even a Skype name.

"From there, it's not hard to see if we have friends or acquaintances in common. I'm obviously not going to come up with a link every time, but odds are I'll find something useful. A couple of months ago I saw on LinkedIn that my prospect graduated from Wharton in 1993. So I flipped an e-mail to Maxine Ladner, who went there more or less at the same time. Bingo, a mutual acquaintance."

Steve had been amazed at how easy it was to find out about people—and a little concerned. "I don't know. It feels uncomfortable to me. What about privacy?"

"I thought that way too at first. But think about it. People put out their information voluntarily, at least most of them. They want to be connected, just like I do. I'm not tapping anyone's phone, just using information they've provided."

"So, more than anything else, you're looking for mutual contacts."

"Right. And once I've got those, I make a few phone calls. If you have a reputation for integrity, people are usually glad to help. Wouldn't you want to connect people if you thought both parties would benefit?"

Connections are powerful. Even if it's not a direct business referral, most people will say yes to your request for a meeting if you can make them aware of a connection they have with you. Almost any connection can be of value—personal, community, school-related, even coincidental. Being rigorous about searching for and cultivating the seeds that can result in a yes to your meeting request is an essential discipline of the sales process. Every salesperson knows it. No meeting, no sale.

Your Business Radar

The next most common strategy for getting a yes to your request for a meeting is using your business radar—keeping your antenna tuned to possibilities. Any conversation, anywhere, can lead to a potentially fruitful connection.

You're introduced to an interesting person at a conference happy hour. You strike up a conversation and agree to get together.

Your plane has been delayed and you get into a conversation with a fellow traveler who's from the city you're about to visit. He tells you one of his friends might be interested in what you do.

You meet another soccer mom at a game and fall into a conversation about your work. It turns out she's a designer for a start-up that could use your services.

Each and every person you meet holds the potential of an unexpected connection—either business or personal, and sometimes both. These connections, both expected and unexpected, are around us all the time, just waiting to be discovered. That's the reason Matt doesn't make cold calls. He doesn't have to.

Asking for the Meeting—What Not to Do

Some of our most important and lasting lessons are the negative ones. Jane will never forget learning how not to ask for that crucial first meeting.

It was during Jane's first several months in sales. She'd performed reasonably well, going out on co-calls with experienced sales pros, learning the ropes, and even closing a few small deals of her own. She had been working on her first big solo deal. She'd met with her prospective client, Roy Westhead, on three separate occasions. Roy was considering proposals from three suppliers. And though Jane sensed she'd made a good impression, she hadn't heard back from Roy since the final presentation, two weeks previously.

Then the call came. "Jane, Roy Westhead here. Congratulations. We liked your proposal, and we liked your style. We'd like to do business with you. My lawyers will mark up the draft contract from your proposal, and we'll have it in your hands by the end of the week."

She was elated, thrilled, and scared all at once. She told Roy how pleased she was and that she would make herself available if there were any questions. Roy thanked her, said he was looking forward to the relationship, and hung up.

Jane remembered standing by her desk, just breathing. Then she almost exploded out of her cube, telling everyone within earshot. High fives went up all around. She was pumped, she was proud, and she was letting out two weeks' worth of tension. She'd seen other salespeople spike the ball into the end zone, and had been envious. Now it was her turn.

Before she knew it her boss approached, smiling a big smile. "Way to go, Jane, I just heard. Nice work."

Jane tried to contain her enthusiasm. "Good news travels fast. But it's not closed yet."

"Don't I know it. But you don't close business until the client decides to work with you. And it sounds like Westhead did just that. I'm not saying the paperwork will take care of itself, but if Westhead himself is on board, I'd say congratulations are in order."

Back in her cubicle, Jane could feel the energy of the office returning to its normal rhythm. But she could still feel her pulse thrumming in her neck, and she couldn't stop smiling. She remembered something she'd read in a novel that featured a salesman who said always put a smile on your face when you talk to your clients, even on the phone. People can hear a smile.

Well, Jane had a smile on her face—and not a phony one either. Why not use it? Why not call that prospective client she'd been trying to get up the gumption to contact? She was too jazzed to do anything else anyway. She dialed Seward's number.

"Ellen Seward."

Jane was surprised to get Ellen on the phone on the first ring. "Ellen, good morning, how are you today? It's Jane Anders calling from Hammer."

"Hi, Jane. What can I do for you?"

"Ellen, I'm calling because I think it would make sense for us to get together."

"Oh, why's that?"

"Because I'm working with a number of firms like yours, and I think there's a good chance I can help you as well."

"I'm not sure I understand."

"Well, I imagine the challenges my clients are facing are similar to yours."

"As in?"

"Well, that's what I'd like to get together and discuss. I want to understand your business, so I can help you."

"Look, Jane, I'm sure you do, but I gotta go. If you're coming to Cincinnati and you have something specific you want to discuss, call, and we'll see. Thanks."

"Okay, Ellen, umm, thanks for your time." Jane heard the disconnect before she finished her sentence.

Jane felt all the air seeping out of her balloon. She'd been feeling elated, invincible. But getting a yes from Ellen required a lot more than a smile in her voice. She needed a thought in her head. And she called before she had one. A hard lesson learned.

Never call a prospect if you have nothing to say. Just touching base or going with the energy of the moment may feel like a good idea, but it isn't. Ellen's inevitable "As in?" needed a response, and Jane didn't have one. If she'd given it some thought, she might easily have had something relevant to offer, such as, "We've been working on strategies for the new tax proposals," or, "We have shipping routes that pass empty trucks by two of your plants on their way to St. Louis," or, "Our analysts are looking at some potential industry disruptions that might be significant to you." Anything that established Jane as useful. The smile in her voice wasn't enough. And as a result, Ellen's answer was no.

Even worse, a no to a request for a meeting isn't just a one-time no. Remember what Matt said about how useful it is for a client to *dis*qualify a salesperson. Once a client has blown you off, whether for good reason or not, you need a *really* good reason to call again. Keep calling without one, and you run the risk of being a sales pest who just won't get the message.

Asking for the Meeting—Increasing the Odds

The first rule for that first call is: *Always have something useful to say.* We recommend a five-step process for requesting a meeting.

1. Find a connection. If you can, arrange for a business referral to send a note in advance to your prospect. At the very least, find some other connection. It can be a person, a shared community, a common interest. Give your potential client a reason to say yes.

2. Rehearse (really *rehearse,* don't just read it to yourself) one or two of your short, relevant scripts that say a little about you and your company. If possible, make them newsworthy, topical, and interesting.

3. Have your calendar handy so you can quickly pinpoint available dates and times for a meeting. Similarly, have an alternate convenient meeting location in mind, in case your client prefers to meet out of their office. This won't happen often, but if it does, you'll make a more professional impression if you're prepared.

4. Have a notepad at hand so you can jot down important information, including names, times, dates, questions clients may ask, and followup questions you may have for them.

5. Make the call. Jane has a rule of calling before ten A.M., because in her experience her contacts' days can get very busy after that. Here's what to say, depending on whether you get a voice mail or a live answer to your call.

If you get your prospect's voice mail, leave a brief message identifying yourself, stating the purpose of your call, and giving a call-back number. (If you have *not* been able to find a connection between you and your potential client, say you think it might be useful to meet because you've helped others in their industry.)

If you get a live answer, have your script ready, and explain who referred you and why. If your prospect asks how you helped the referring contact, say something like, "We worked together to analyze his situation and design a solution. [Referring contact] was pleased, which is why he was willing to refer me to you." Obviously, your dealings are confidential, so you can't reveal details. If your client presses for more information about how you can help them, follow up by referring to generic problems faced by similar firms, especially ones you've helped mitigate, and then add, "My experience is that no two businesses are completely alike, so canned solutions aren't useful. I like to help people uncover areas where we can be useful. If you don't have any of those, there's no reason to meet. But that would be unusual. I've never found an organization that couldn't earn more, or spend less, or improve its working environment in some way. I have a very brief process that helps identify where I might offer value. That's what [referring contact] and I did together. And I'd be happy to do it with you. If we can't find a way to be useful to you, we'll both have learned something." Then offer to make an appointment.

Of course, this five-step approach doesn't always work, but it's a lot more likely to succeed than Jane's call to Ellen Seward.

Finally, if your client still says no, leave the door open and end your call with a question. "I understand. There just don't seem to be enough hours in the day. Would it be okay if I gave you a ring in a few months? Or if I hear of something that might affect your business? If issues come up for you, I think there's a good chance I can offer help. I promise to be respectful of your time."

Don't Take Our Word for It, Try It Yourself

Make a list of ten companies you'd like to meet with in the next six months. You'll find their names through conferences, associations, trade magazines, lists your company has, the grapevine, and the Internet.

Do a basic Google search to find individuals within those companies. Then do quick Google, Facebook, LinkedIn, Twitter, and Skype searches on those people. See what comes up. It won't take long to discover that some play hockey, some quilt, and some are in theatrical productions. People do things. That's where they meet and interact with other people.

Next, ask yourself, "What might be all the ways I can be (or already am) connected to this person?" Then make a list of possible answers. Don't judge them out of existence (remember the principle of separating your thinking in chapter 2). Just list them. After you've made a long list, review it, and then select the most viable, practical, or promising approaches.

One of those approaches will be through your own network of colleagues and friends. Ask them if they know, or know about, the person you want to meet, or if they know anyone else in that person's organization. Just putting out a simple message to people you know ("I need a connection to Jim Ripley at Baton Financial so he'll say yes to my request for a meeting. I'd appreciate any ideas") will usually net you a connection, sooner or later.

Once you have identified the people you want to contact and the connections you have with them, find ways to make them aware of how you are connected *before your call*. If you have a mutual friend, associate, history, or interest, let your prospect know in an e-mail, through a social network, or even through your mutual acquaintance, if possible. Your goal is to make your prospect aware of the connection before you call so you are no longer a stranger. But your preparation doesn't end there. Once you've highlighted your connection, you also need to figure out what you want to say in your initial phone call—something they might find interesting or useful, a challenge they might face, something they may want to hear more about. If you do this well, your prospective clients should have two reasons to say yes to your meeting request—they have a connection with you, and they're intrigued about what you may have to offer.

U ltimately, there's no need to make cold calls. In order to ask for a meeting with a reasonable expectation you'll get it, you need just two things: a connection and a reason. In today's interconnected world, a connection shouldn't be hard to find. The reason is up to you.

Why might someone be willing to hear more about what you have to offer? Dozens of reasons. Here's a starter list.

YOUR NETWORK

- You have been referred by someone relevant to your client's work: in the best case, they've sent an e-mail mentioning you.
- You are part of a shared professional network: someone in your organization knows someone in theirs.
- You work with well-known companies or people (use caution—overt name-dropping can backfire).
- You have connections with people who might be useful to them.
- You know people in common outside of work.

YOUR COMPANY

- You can execute faster or better than your competitors: your product or service is demonstrably better.
- You have capabilities your client is unaware of: "One reason I want to meet you is to let you know our total range of capabilities. One of them may be useful to you."

YOUR BUSINESS SAVVY

- You offer interesting insights on your client's situation.
- You have relevant intelligence that relates to an initiative your client is pursuing or to industry trends.
- You are a known problem solver and innovative thinker.
- You work with your client's competitors or companies in their supply or delivery chain.
- You have other experience in their business niche.

SERENDIPITY

- You're going to be in your client's neighborhood or city.

CHAPTER 9

Make Research Make Sense— Find Five Questions

To understand is hard. Once one understands, action is easy.

—Sun Yat-sen

Once you have your scripts in hand and you've gotten a yes to your request for a meeting, you need to organize your resources to ensure your meeting will be as productive as possible—for both you and your potential client. And that means research.

A lot of salespeople wince at the thought. They see research as a painful chore—a kind of black hole that will suck up their time and energy, producing little in return. But *not* doing research for your meeting is like not stretching before a 10k race. You won't perform at your peak, and you risk pulling up with an injury long before the finish line. Whether you research or not, you're going to be investing a lot of yourself in a meeting that will last only an hour or so. How you perform in that hour can make the difference between an outcome to celebrate or an outcome that has you kicking yourself for not being sufficiently prepared. Productive Selling isn't magic. It takes work. Part of that work is your premeeting research. And the good news is, research doesn't have to be a black hole. In fact, it doesn't have to be hard at all.

With the right approach and the right tools, you can do your research quickly, efficiently, and effectively. You'll find that your research not only provides facts and figures but leads you to insights about your client's business that can differentiate you from the many other people vying for their time and attention. And who knows, you might even enjoy it!

The Goal of Research

The more you know about your client, their organizations, and the environment in which they operate, the better you'll be able to understand what they tell you during your meeting. In other words, the more intelligence you gather, the more intelligent you can be. The more intelligent you are about your client's world, the more credibility you can earn and the more likely you'll be able to offer them real value.

But what about that black hole? You can't research forever. So how do you know when you've done enough?

The answer is to target four clear objectives for your research:

- Provide basic background for a productive conversation
- Help you establish credibility
- Create a structure for your meeting, specifically five areas you want to explore
- Begin to develop ideas that offer value to your client

Background

You need to be able to talk knowledgeably about your client's company, their industry, and the environment in which they operate. You also need to have enough context to understand what they tell you. The specific information you need will vary from industry to industry, but a good starting point is the basic list on page 82.*

---

*The list is not exhaustive. Every company and every industry will have their own way of viewing themselves. Design a basic statistical checklist that works for the clients you need to sell to.

- What are their core products or services?
- Who are their markets?
- Who are their competitors?
- What strategic alliances do they have?
- Where do they operate?
- Where do they manufacture?
- How profitable have they been over the past several years?

- How many employees do they have?
- What is their market capitalization?
- What is their relationship to your market?
- What is their relationship to your competitors?
- Has your company done business with them before? What were the results?

Ideally, you should be able to assemble a brief company and industry profile. If you are new to the industry, ask your colleagues to suggest additional information that might be important. Over time, meeting with people from similar sectors, you'll get a sense of the minimum you need to know to have a productive conversation.

Credibility

Your background research will go a long way toward helping you establish credibility, but there's more to do. As we'll discuss in chapter 15, you will be spending the first part of your meeting establishing enough credibility for your client to feel comfortable answering your questions. To cross the credibility threshold you need not just information but insight. That means you'll want to find out things about the company or industry that may be below the surface. It may be useful, for example, to research questions like: What is the general health of their industry? What are the key industry trends? Who writes about the industry, and what do they say? Who are the key individuals in the company? Who in your own organization might have useful perspectives or insights about the company or its industry? What are they? As you conduct your research, keep asking yourself, "Do I know enough to be credible?"

Ideally, in your meeting, you want your client to be thinking, "This person really gets it, really gets us."

Structure

Research doesn't always mean finding answers. In fact, one of your most important research objectives is to find questions. As we will discuss in chapter 16, a core principle of Productive Selling is to structure your meeting around the questions you ask about your client's situation, needs, and challenges. Your research should help you design those questions.

Your goal is to come up with five areas of questioning that you plan to explore in your face-to-face meeting. Why five? Planning to explore only one or two areas is often not enough. If they run dry, you'll want to have something else to ask about. On the other hand, ten areas are probably too many: it's unlikely you'll have time to explore that much territory in a single meeting. So, for us, five has proven to be the Goldilocks number—not too many, not too few.

Finding those questions can be surprisingly easy. We'll show you our favorite tool for doing that in the next few pages.

Ideas

The final objective of your research is to help you develop ideas that can deliver value to your client. You probably won't deliberately look for these ideas as you research, but they will almost certainly occur to you. As you learn about your client, your brain will automatically start making connections—connections between your client's company and the services you offer, connections between your experience and your client's situation, connections between your client and other people you know. Every one of these connections is an embryonic idea. Note them down. Don't worry at this point if they seem good or bad or smart or off the wall. Just note them down—all of them.

Remember to separate your thinking. If you try to judge your ideas while you generate them, you'll judge most of them out of existence. But if you simply let yourself *have* the ideas, then note them down, and then come back to them later, you'll have more ideas and better ideas to choose from. Don't let a potentially useful idea go to waste. Write it down. You can always revisit your list later and select the ones you want to pursue.

Know Wonder

Know Wonder is one of the most useful tools in the Productive Selling arsenal. It's a deceptively simple way to analyze situations, focus research, and generate the kinds of questions that can turn a run-of-the-mill meeting into a dynamic exchange of ideas. The name of the tool says it all. It asks two simple questions: *What do you know?* and *What do you wonder?*

You can use Know Wonder by yourself, but it's usually more effective if you can get other perspectives as well, so we recommend working with a colleague if you can.

Here's how it works.

Start with a large piece of paper. Divide your page into two columns. Label the left column "Know" and the right column "Wonder." Then, in the left column, list all the things you know about your prospective client, the company, the industry—in other words, anything you know about what you are getting into. Once again, don't judge, just write.

Now, in the right column, list all the things you wonder about your client, the company, the industry, and the environment—in other words, all the things you *don't* yet know, but which might be useful if you did. Use what you know to trigger what you wonder. Write everything and anything that comes to mind.

By the time you've finished, even a brief Know Wonder, you should have a robust list of things you understand about your client and things you need to research further—a useful platform on which to build.

Page 85 shows what a typical Know Wonder sheet might look like after about ten minutes of thinking.

Know	Wonder
• Fosbury just closed production plant in Sandusky.	• Has bad press affected business strategy, community relations?
• Got lots of bad press on that.	• Has fallout impacted John's role or objectives?
• CEO spoke to congressional committee on the subject.	
• Are partnering to build new plant in Chile.	• Why Chile? Has John visited? Any concerns about joint venture?
• Fifth most profitable company in their niche.	• What did CEO say to Congress?
• Have been identified as possible takeover target.	• What divisions could be vulnerable in merger?
• John graduated from U Penn.	• Any products/units that may be shed in merger?
• John used to work at same company as our CFO, were on company bowling team together, which John founded.	• Does John follow U Penn basketball? Were they good when he was there?
	• Does John still bowl? Why did he start the team?

This simple Know Wonder list does two things for you: it gives you a useful context to help you understand your client's situation, and it suggests a wealth of relevant areas to explore. Some of them you can research before your meeting, such as *What did CEO say to Congress? Why choose Chile?* Others may be more appropriate to explore face-to-face with your client, such as *Has fallout impacted John's role or objectives? What divisions could be vulnerable in merger situation? Does John still bowl? Why did he start the team?* (If you happen to be interested in bowling and somehow connected to the bowling world, this last item might be a springboard to a personal relationship; we'll discuss this aspect of your client meeting in chapters 14, 18, and 21.)

In the example above, we've focused on particular situations the company faces. There is also a variety of standard items you'll probably *always* wonder about—things you'll want to know about any client, such as its market value, its total revenues, its stock performance, countries or regions it operates in, relationships with regulators, tax situation, and so on. These fall under the basic background you'll want to have in case they come up in your meeting.

As you fill in the Know column and add to the Wonder column, ideas will pop into your head about how you might be able to help your client. Capture them as and when they occur to you. The more advance thinking you can do about ways you can offer value to your client, the more confident you'll be going into your meeting—and the more alternatives you'll have to adjust to the natural ebbs and flows of your conversation.

We're confident that once you give it a try, you'll find Know Wonder to be an indispensable tool. At first you may think it's almost too simple to be useful, but think of the lowly hammer—about as simple as a tool can get. But have you ever tried to drive a nail without one?

How to Research

Before you even start your premeeting research, you'll already have some information, some leads, and some ideas from the basic research you did to get a yes to your meeting request. Now is the time to explore them further.

There is no single, definitive best place to find information. Every industry and sales organization will have unique requirements. But there are several general sources and approaches that offer a good start. This is the research checklist we use.

- **Google**. It seems redundant even to list this, but it's where we start. And you should too. Some of our colleagues are now using Microsoft's Bing as well, because its integration with Facebook and

Twitter is stronger. Nevertheless, Google is still the king in terms of speed and relevance. Pay particular attention to search results showing newspaper, news site, or business journal articles.

- **Social networks.** As of this writing, the gorilla is still Facebook, but for business relevance, and the ability to access individual résumés, LinkedIn is our favorite, followed closely by Twitter.

- **Web sites.** Once you've found the address for your target organization, its various Web sites can provide you with annual reports, press releases, investor pages, SEC filings, company personnel, boards of directors, product and service offerings, contact numbers and addresses, and even maps to show you how to get there. After you've searched your target company, look up the Web sites of industry associations it belongs to, and of course the Web sites of its competitors.

- **Blogs.** Both companies and the people who work for them have blogs. They're not hard to find (through Google, LinkedIn, and other resources mentioned above). You can learn a lot from the things people write and post about themselves.

- **Annual reports.** Most public companies have these available on their Web sites, but occasionally you may need to access hard copies (yes, they still print them). One salesperson we know buys a few shares of stock in each of his client and future client companies (those that are public). As a shareholder, he gets quarterly and annual reports delivered to his doorstep. The CEO's state-of-the-company message at the front of every report is a must-read, providing useful information on the year in review, company values, and major initiatives and challenges.

- **Your network**. This includes your own team as well as your wider circle of business acquaintances and friends. People know people, and people have histories. You went through the same process to establish one connection to get a yes to your meeting request. You are now doing the same thing in more detail. Don't forget the senior people in your firm. They have more history, have worked in more places, and probably know more people than anyone else in your firm. Use them. Getting the chance to pick the brain of your COO isn't always easy. Your scheduled meetings with her will be rare. But if you work it efficiently, you may be able to get her take on several potential clients at a single session. Her perspective could be invaluable.

Your network—professional or personal, casual or close—can be like your own personal team of Mars Rovers. They know things you don't know, they see things you don't see, they hear things you don't hear, they know people you don't know. More often than not these people are happy to help you (and happy to receive your help when they need it). Ask them. You'll both benefit.

The Truth About Research

The research process above is the one we use. It works for us. Give it a try. Then, over time, evolve your own process, one that fits your style, your business, and your circumstances.

As you become more comfortable and practiced, you'll know when you have enough information for a productive sales meeting. You'll learn how to avoid overresearching and underresearching. You'll naturally tweak and refine your information-gathering process to give you the data you need at a price (in time and effort) that you're willing to pay. We hope you'll take our recommendations as a starting point and design a research process that works for you.

You'll find that once you've merged that process into your routine, research won't be a separate activity anymore. It will be something you naturally integrate into almost all your activities. It will become what's known as an unconscious competency, like riding a bike without even thinking about it.

You'll establish a routine, perhaps every Tuesday morning over coffee, when you read the trades to keep up to date on industry trends. If you have a handful of future clients identified, your radar will be tuned to any article that mentions them or relates to a situation that impacts them. You'll read an article about one company in your sector, and you'll automatically flag information that may be useful for getting a meeting with another.

You'll automatically trawl for new leads to clients, discovering connections and doing research for upcoming meetings all at the same time. If you know your next meeting has holdings in Texas, and you see an article on pending legislation there, you'll flag it as an area to explore, or even a chance to offer your client some additional value in the form of a contact or a relevant tip.

Once you're tuned in, every conversation you have and article you read is research. Like buying a new car and suddenly seeing that same model everywhere you drive, you'll see information that relates to your clients and prospective clients almost everywhere.

In fact, your biggest challenge may be capturing and organizing all the data you start discovering. We use a simple, free-form database called Evernote. It lives in the cloud, so your files can be with you anywhere, anytime—on your phone, your computer, or your tablet. See an article online? Clip it from your browser into Evernote. Read something offline? Snap a picture and dump it automatically into Evernote (which can even search photographed text). Tag, group, and search by company, by industry, by person, by date, by place, by anything. Then, when it comes time to ask for that meeting with that company you've been eyeing, you'll have a head start.

As we said in the beginning of this chapter, mention research and a lot of salespeople start running for the hills. But research is essential. And it can be easy. Every organization, and every person in it, has a story. In those stories are the keys to connecting with them. Your research is the fuel, your curiosity the match. Together, they ignite your enthusiasm to discover the unexpected connections that can be the beginnings of a relationship. That's what productive salespeople do.

CHAPTER 10

Raise the BAR—Set Success Criteria

How will you know you've reached your goal
if you don't know what it looks like?

—Virgil

Steve and Virgil met in their usual haunt. Same place, same booth, probably even the same toothpicks.

"So how's the nim sequence coming?" asked Virgil.

"Good. I was already fairly solid in my scripts. They're probably the only thing that saved me from complete disaster in that meeting with Ian, but I refined them, and I think they're better now."

"How so?"

"Well, they're shorter, for one. They get to the point faster. They're also more targeted. One key point per script. And I've made them more people-oriented, not just facts and figures."

"Sounds good. Anything else?"

"Yeah, in a funny way the biggest thing is not so much the scripts themselves but just knowing I have them. Kind of like a confidence factor, I think. Like the automatic data backups we have at work. You might not ever need them, but you feel better knowing they're there."

"So what's next?"

"I'm still waiting for that Before Action Review we talked about last time. According to the toothpicks, that's where we are now."

"You have a client?"

"Not yet," Steve said, smiling, "but I have a meeting."

"Excellent! Tell me about it."

Steve gave Virgil a quick rundown of his success in getting the new meeting—with a company called Axel, a competitor of Ian's. He was optimistic about it because he now saw his unsuccessful meeting with Ian as a kind of dry run for the upcoming session. Based on his talks with Matt and Jane, he had a better feel for what to do and, more important, what not to do. He certainly wouldn't be making assumptions based on a previous relationship. He'd had one with Ian, but Axel was virgin territory.

"Let's go, then." Virgil reached over and slid Steve's notepad so they could both see it easily, then flipped to a blank page. "This is probably going to be a lot more straightforward than you thought."

Virgil turned the notepad lengthwise and drew five columns. He labeled each one with a letter: D, R, I, V, and E.

D	R	I	V	E

"The main purpose of a Before Action Review is to establish success criteria. It's not a detailed plan of action. But what it does is give you a way of setting out what you want to achieve, so you have a way of evaluating how you did after it's all over. That's the After Action Review we talked about."

"That makes sense. You have to know where you want to go so you can tell if you got there."

"Right. That's all it is—a way of letting you know what you're going to measure in the end. And one of the simplest tools to do that is something called DRIVE. Each letter stands for one of the factors that's going to make up your success—or not."

Virgil explained the chart he was drawing. DRIVE was an acronym of the questions he was going to ask for each column.

D stands for Desired outcomes. In the case of a sales meeting, what do you want the meeting to do for you and for your client?

R stands for Risks. What are the possible outcomes of the meeting that you want to avoid?

I stands for Investment. What are you prepared to invest in the sales effort? What resources, what time, what research? Would you be happy to meet the same client ten times to make the sale? Or would it start to become uneconomical at that point? What are your not-to-exceeds?

V stands for Vision and Values. Who do you want your client to know you are as a result of your interaction? How will your vision or your values be conveyed by what you say and what you do?

E stands for Essential outcomes. What are the key, observable, measurable outcomes of the meeting that will indicate success? This is more precise than the Desired outcomes in the first column. You may *want* certain outcomes, but the outcomes in this fifth column are the ones that are absolutely necessary in order for you to consider your meeting a success.

DRIVE is an easy-to-remember and easy-to-use tool that can quickly give you a solid sense of what a successful endeavor will look like and feel like. We'll be using it here to set success criteria for a sales meeting, but you could also use it to establish success criteria for an entire sales campaign—or, in the case of OPFOR, a military training exercise.

DRIVE is a powerful tool that allows you to establish success criteria for almost any activity, and it can be particularly useful as a Before Action Review for a sales meeting. Let's see how Steve and Virgil use it.

Steve was intrigued. "So you use this DRIVE tool before any action you take?"

"Not any action, no. But if I want to be able to evaluate it usefully at the end, it's a good idea to do a DRIVE. You can do it formally, like we will now, or you can just run through it in your head, but one way or another, if you plan to measure how effective an action was, you have to create some benchmarks to measure it against; in other words, your criteria for success. That's what DRIVE is for."

"Can we do one for my upcoming meting with Axel?"

"That's what I'm here for. Just a word of caution, though. You may not have all the information you need with you just now, but that's okay, we'll make a start, and if there are any blanks you can fill them in later. So, what's your D, your Desired outcomes for the meeting?"

Steve picked up the pencil and started writing. "Well, that's easy. I want to make the sale."

Virgil put his hand on Steve's forearm. "Whoa, Steve. For sure you want to make the sale, but in the first meeting?"

"Well, no, you're right, that would be unlikely. It'll take three meetings, at least, plus several contacts in between. But you said not to judge. So if you want me to list my *desired* outcomes, one would be to walk out of my meeting with a sale."

Virgil smiled. "Touché. You're getting it. That's exactly what you should be doing. Write down everything and anything that occurs to you. We can shorten your lists later. Part of that shortening might be to parse out some items into two different DRIVE sheets, one for your first meeting, and the other for the sales process with Axel as a whole. But right now, all we want is to capture everything. Great. Keep going."

After ten minutes, page 94 shows what Steve's DRIVE looked like.

Steve was surprised at how much he'd gotten down in such a short time. "That didn't take long."

"It usually doesn't. It's just that people don't do it. Ten, twenty, maybe thirty minutes on this end can save you a lot of agony at the other end. But let's not get too self-congratulatory just yet. You've got a good list, but the job's not done yet. You have to decide which items are really important."

"Well, they all are. I mean, even though you told me not to be judgmental at this stage, it looks to me like every one of these things would be a success indicator."

"Fair enough, but there are too many different items for the list to be

Desired Outcomes	Risks to Avoid	Investment Not to Exceed	Vision or Values	Essential Outcomes
· Make the sale	· Talking too much	· 2 hours basic research (for first meeting.)	· Usefulness	· Establish usefulness
· Discover client's needs	· Losing focus		· Listener	· Demostrate understanding
· Establish creditability quickly	· Addressing wrong problem	· Premeet with Brad + Gary	· Trustworthy	· Offer help
· Get followup meeting	· Not getting followup meeting	· Presentation budget $2K	· Problem solver	· Make at least one promise
· Learn who makes buying decisons	· Not getting followup meeting	· 4 meetings? Maybe 5? More?	· Friendly	
· Understand client's contracting process		· Deal within 4 months?	· Success together	· Schedule followup meeting (with decision maker if needed)
· Find personal followup opportunity			· Reliable	
· Find business followup opportunity			· Competent	

useful to you. What you need is to pick a number of key items, usually fewer than ten, that if you achieved, you'd consider your meeting a success—and if not, less than a success."

"I get your point about too many success indicators. I can't afford to be analyzing forever. I've got my day job to do too. But looking at the list, it seems like there isn't anything on it I wouldn't want to achieve, is there?"

Virgil picked up the pencil and used it as a pointer. "Okay, let's start with the first item, 'Make the sale.' I know you'd be delighted to do that in your first meeting . . ."

"Over the moon!" Steve interjected.

"But if you don't, would the meeting be a failure?"

"Well, no. Like I said, it would be pretty unlikely in one meeting."

"Right, so you could say that would be nice to have, but not necessary to have in order for you to consider the meeting a success. So the first thing we want to do now is look for those items that really would be the difference between success and not success, at least from your point of view."

"From my point of view?"

"Sure, this is your meeting. You're the one who has to set the success criteria. They might be very different for another salesman, but for you, you need to define what success is—and isn't—to you."

"Okay, but there's still something that bothers me. What about all these overlaps and duplication? I mean, I've got the words *followup meeting* in here at least five times."

"Which means?"

"Which means it's important, I guess."

"Dead on. One of the things that's so useful about DRIVE is that it tends to highlight those things that are important. They start popping out at you, usually because they get repeated. It's a lot better to be redundant at this stage than to miss something. The key is suspending your judgment, just what you said when you started to make the list. By not judging whether something should or shouldn't be on the list, you'll find yourself coming back to those key items over and over. And that tells you something."

"The more often it's on the list, the more important it is."

"Usually. Or maybe there's another reason. Maybe it's something you're particularly worried about or distracted about. But for whatever reason, the fact that you're repeating it means it deserves to be looked at closely."

For the next twenty minutes, they went over the five lists, Virgil challenging Steve on each item. If he wanted to keep it, why? If he wanted to delete it, why? In the end, page 96 shows what Steve's highlighted DRIVE looked like.

Desired Outcomes	Risks to Avoid	Investment Not to Exceed	Vision or Values	Essential Outcomes
· Make the sale	· Talking too much	· 2 hours basic research (for first meeting)	· Usefulness	· Establish usefulness
· Discover client's needs	· Losing focus	· Premeet with Brad + Gary	· Listener	· Demostrate understand-ing
· Establish creditability quickly	· Addressing wrong problem	· Presentation budget $2K	· Trust-worthy	· Offer help
· Get followup meeting	· Not getting followup meeting	· 4 meetings? Maybe 5? More?	· Problem solver	· Make at least one promise
· Learn who makes buying decisons		· Deal within 4 months?	· Friendly	· Schedule followup meeting (with decision maker if needed)
· Understand client's contracting process			· Success together	
· Find personal followup opportunity			· Reliable	
· Find business followup opportunity			· Competent	

Steve agreed that all the items were important, but that the ones they had highlighted were the most significant. After combining and rationalizing the repeated items, Steve determined that the success criteria for his first meeting with Axel should be as follows:

He would have to *discover his client's needs.* Clearly, without that, he wouldn't be able to get much further.

If he was going to uncover his client's needs, he would have to ask good questions and listen to his client's answers. As obvious as it might seem, success would require him to *establish himself as a credible questioner and a good listener.* And that meant he would have to keep a lid on his tendency to talk too much, no matter how excited he got about what his company had to offer.

After uncovering his client's needs, he would have to *establish himself as a problem solver,* someone who could genuinely offer value.

All the items in the Essential outcomes column seemed important. Steve needed to *demonstrate an understanding* of Axel's situation and challenges and to *demonstrate his usefulness* in addressing those issues. In order to do that, he'd have to be able to *offer help,* maybe not even through his product but perhaps in some other way, for example by offering an insight or a connection. In turn, that would require *making and keeping a promise* of some sort—something as simple as sending his client useful information or referring him to a possible business contact. And most important, he had to be sure to get some kind of *followup meeting*—a business followup for sure, but if he could also get a personal touch point with his client, that would be even better.

As to the item in the Investment column, Steve reluctantly admitted that though it wasn't a deal killer, *keeping his presentation budget below two thousand dollars* was important. He'd agreed on this maximum with his partners. If he got Axel to sign, the excess cost would be overlooked, but if he didn't, an overbudget presentation could become a sore point.

In the end, Steve distilled his success criteria for the first meeting to seven items.

- Establish credibility to question (then listen well)
- Discover client's needs
- Demonstrate problem-solving capabilities
- Demonstrate usefulness by offering help
- Make (and keep) a promise
- Stay within budget
- Get followup meeting

When they finished their lunch, Steve said, "Wow, I really feel I have a good handle on what I have to do now. I'm kind of amazed. I've never done anything like this before."

"People usually don't. That's why OPFOR almost always wins. They establish their measures of success in the Before Action Review, they determine how well they did in the After Action Review, and then they try to learn from their experience. Not that complicated really." He slid the check over to Steve. "Worth the lunch?"

"You bet," said Steve as he reached for his wallet.

CHAPTER 11

The Weakest Ink—Make Your Notes Sing

The weakest ink is better than the strongest memory.

—Chinese proverb

The verb *to note* means to notice or pay attention to something.

When you *take notes,* you enhance your ability to remember what you've noticed.

When you use *speaking notes,* you both remind yourself of what you want to say and create a structure for your presentation. Your speaking notes are, in effect, a blend of content and process—what you want to say in the meeting and the structure you'll use to do so.

If you get better at paying attention, remembering what you notice, and structuring your sales meetings, you will get better at selling. That's why we recommend the Q-Notes approach. It's a way to help you strengthen all three of these Productive Selling skills—noticing, remembering, and structuring.

Really? With notes?

Really. Sometimes the simplest tools are the most powerful—like the Know Wonder tool for clarifying your research needs in chapter 9 and the DRIVE tool for establishing success criteria in chapter 10.

First, some perspective: no matter how good your memory is, it isn't good enough. Think about the last time you were at a party. On the way home you might have said to your partner, "You know, that Pat is a really good guy."

Your partner might have said, "I didn't get to talk to him much. What makes you say that?"

"I dunno. He just seemed interesting—and funny."

"What did he say?"

You think harder about your conversation. What were the specific things he said that gave you the favorable impression? You start to reply, but nothing concrete comes. You can't offer any real evidence.

Sound familiar? Don't worry, it's not just you. It's all of us. We're generally a lot better at remembering our impressions of people than the specific things they said that gave us those impressions. The feelings stick. The data doesn't.

That's not a big problem in a party situation. But it can ruin your day in a sales situation.

It's critically important that you capture what you learn in a meeting *as you learn it*, so you can review it for later followup, and mine it for ideas that didn't occur to you at the time. What doesn't get recorded quickly fades from memory and becomes less and less useful. Guaranteed.

So you need a tool that sharpens your ability to observe and makes it easy to recall what you noticed. Most good salespeople will agree that taking good notes is the best way to capture the key points of your conversation so you can recall and review them later.

But what if this thinking is backward? What if the *way* you take notes could enhance your ability to observe what's most important? What if you had a way to take notes that allowed you to maintain focus on your client instead of madly scribbling down details? What if you could take notes so smoothly that nobody even noticed? And what if your notes were so accurate that you could recall the most specific details of the most important information?

What if instead of the conversation driving the notes, your notes drove the conversation?

Here's how to achieve all those things simply, repeatedly, and reliably: Q-Notes. You can use Q-Notes to structure your meetings, capture key thoughts, keep focused on what's important, and provide a treasure trove of followup material—for both you and your client—after the meeting is over.

We call them Q-Notes because you divide your page into four quadrants. Remember: your notes aren't just for recording information. You'll also use them to actually *structure* your meeting, so you can also think of the *Q* in Q-Notes as the word *cue*. Your Q-Notes are designed to cue you about what you want to say—whether they're statements or questions—throughout the meeting. The Q-Notes approach allows you to structure the information you *receive* into four useful areas that make it easier to record and remember what was said—and then structure what *you* want to communicate by giving you cues. It's like speaking notes for what you want to say—and when.

The Q-Note Template

The Q-Note template divides your notes into four equally important categories: questions you want to ask during the meeting (Quad 1), ideas you want to deliver at the end of the meeting (Quad 2), things you discover about your client during the meeting (Quad 3), and ideas for followup activities after the meeting (Quad 4).

There's a blank Q-Notes template on page 102.

You can see that the top left quadrant (Quad 1) becomes a structure or agenda for the meeting. The top right quadrant (Quad 2) becomes a place to record ideas that deliver value to the client at the end of the meeting. The bottom left quadrant (Quad 3) becomes a place to record observations about the client's interests, issues, and needs. And the bottom right quadrant (Quad 4) is a checklist of opportunities for following up with the client after the meeting.

By organizing your notes visually on the page, you'll find you need to write less, and you'll be able to decipher them more easily later. Writing down one or two key words should be sufficient to trigger your memory later on.

	Discovery	Delivery
During Meeting	Agenda Quadrant Q1	Value Quadrant Q2
After Meeting	Key Information Q3	Follow up Checklist Q4

Here's how we suggest you use the Q-Notes template:

Quad 1—Top Left (fill in before and during meeting)

Record the questions you want to ask. These are the five areas you flagged in your research that you thought would be useful to explore in your sales conversation. Phrase these as Who, What, Where, When, Why, or How questions. Or use the lead-in "Tell me more about . . ." During the meeting, as you uncover new areas to explore, add relevant questions here to remind you of what to return to later in the meeting.

When you've explored an area to your satisfaction, and generated ideas that might be helpful to your client, choose another area to explore. You might choose one of the five from your research, or one you added as you listened to your client.

Whenever the conversation lulls, or you've explored one topic enough, peek at this quadrant of your Q-Notes, choose a new topic you're curious about, and ask a new question, such as, "Let me ask you a question about your push into the Canadian market. . . ." Make sure you have enough of these so that when you run dry, you'll always have something to say. (That's why we suggested in chapter 9 that one of the goals of your research should be to identify five areas of questioning you want to explore in the face-to-face meeting.)

Quad 2—Top Right (fill in before and during meeting)

This is the value quadrant. It's where you list the ideas for helping your client that you've uncovered during your research, and it's where you note any new ideas that occur to you while listening to your client—how your product or service can help, people they should know, and resources you can help them access. The new ideas you discover during your meeting may well trump the ones you had during your research. You may find that you never even mention the ideas from your premeeting research because you generate better ones during your conversation. We'll discuss later, in chapter 16, the importance of *not* articulating these thoughts right away while you're still exploring with your client. The key is to write them down here in the top right quadrant, so you can bring them up later in the meeting when they'll be most useful to both you and your client.

Quad 3—Bottom Left (fill in during meeting)

During your meeting, you'll often find that your client's answers will stimulate new questions to explore later in the meeting. If so, you've noted them in Quad 1. Sometimes, however, you'll learn something important that doesn't need to be explored in the meeting—or that you're not ready to explore yet. Perhaps you need off-line time to think about it before you can handle the issue credibly, or you'd like to consult someone else in your network first, or the meeting is just getting squeezed for time. These are the kinds of items you note in Quad 3, so you can refer to them after your meeting.

Quad 3 is also where you note personal information—perhaps something you learned during the informal start of the meeting, such as, "skier Mt. Blanc, 3 kids, daughter @ NYU, coaches Little League, Pebble Beach." This informal information can offer opportunities for further meetings, lubricate future conversations, and form the basis for authentic touch points for developing a relationship.

Quad 4—Bottom Right (fill in during and after meeting)

Quad 4 is your followup quadrant, where you'll record opportunities for further contact with your client. Perhaps they're speaking at a conference in two weeks, or the team they coach has an upcoming championship game, or they mentioned they were curious about the new reporting regulations the government just published. Almost any information in Quad 3 might be an opportunity for followup contact. The same goes for the ideas in Quad 2 that you didn't get a chance to explore further during the meeting. Note them here.

Writing Helps Only If You Can Read It

As powerful as the Q-Notes template is, your notes will be useless to you if you can't read them. That means you must—this is one of those few absolutes we said we'd give you—you *must* learn to write legibly without focusing on your page. It's an essential sales skill. One way to do this is to develop your own, reproducible shorthand. It's easier to write short forms than complete words and sentences while keeping focus on your client. You just need enough to remember the point for a few hours. So take the time to develop—and practice—a set of common abbreviations, symbols, codes, or hieroglyphics that will be instantly meaningful to *you* (it doesn't matter if others can interpret them).

	Discovery	Delivery
During Meeting	This is the agenda quadrant. Here you'll write questions to ask in the meeting, based on the five areas you identified in your research. These questions will usually start with Who, What, Where, Why, or How, or simply "Tell me more about . . ." For example, "You're expanding into the Canadian market. What issues have you encountered that are different from your U.S. operations?" During the meeting, as you uncover other areas to explore note here new questions that occur to you so you can return to them later in the meeting. **Q1**	This is the value quadrant. Here you'll note ideas and suggestions you generated before the meeting to help your client. For example, you might offer to connect them with a Quebecois translation service you've used. During the meeting, new ideas will occur to you while listening to your client—how your product or service can help, people they should know, and resources you can help them access. Note these additional ideas here too. **Q2**
After Meeting	This is the key information quadrant. Here you'll note information you may not want to explore during the meeting but which may be useful later. This can be either business related or personal—anything that might provide an opportunity for a future touch point. For example, something you learned during the informal start of the meeting, such as "skier—Mt. Blanc, 3 kids, daughter @ NYU, coaches Little League, Pebble Beach." **Q3**	This is the followup checklist quadrant. Here you can note almost any idea in Quad 3 (left) or Quad 2 (above) that might offer a chance for a followip conversation. For example, you learned that your client is speaking at a conference in two weeks, or that the team he coaches has an upcoming championship game, or that the company might be concerned about new reporting regulations the government just published. **Q4**

What About Three Weeks from Now?

It's one thing to be able to interpret your notes on the spot, or even a few hours later, while your meeting is still fresh in your mind. It's quite another to try to do so days, weeks, or months later. So here's another absolute rule: *Always schedule time as soon as possible after your meeting (within an hour or two at most) to rewrite your meeting notes in detail. Always.* Consider the time it takes to do this as part of your meeting time. Consider it part of the investment you make in yourself and your sales process (when you do your DRIVE). Consider it indispensable. This applies not only to the information you hear in the meeting but also to your own insights and ideas. Don't fool yourself; as brilliant as they might seem while you're having them, you won't remember them later. So rewrite your notes as completely as you can, as soon as you can. Always remember this Jewish proverb: "For five seconds you're a genius, the rest of your life an idiot—write it down!"

Q-Notes—A Multipurpose Tool

- Your Q-Notes are your exploration agenda—the five key questions you designed based on your research. These questions become a kind of structural tree on which to hang your meeting.
- Your Q-Notes help you orchestrate an efficient and effective meeting. They allow you to return smoothly to areas of discussion with followup questions. They also give you a place to record the long list of ideas you'll want to offer your client during the later stages of the meeting.
- Your Q-Notes allow you to record a solid set of followup opportunities. You'll be able to mine them for client information and issues, both personal and professional, that you can use to build a relationship over time. (We discuss debriefing your meeting in chapter 21.)

You'll be able to do all this while still maintaining focus on your client because the Q-Notes template lets you record maximum information with minimum writing.

But the value of Q-Notes isn't restricted to sales meetings. Like many of the other Productive Selling tools we recommend in this book, Q-Notes are useful for countless other business and personal situations. Making a service call? Make a better one by structuring and recording it with your Q-Notes. Delivering a short presentation at the office or to your service club? Q-Notes can help you make a better one. Conducting a performance review? Be a better coach with Q-Notes. Planning a meal? Use your Q-Notes template for your shopping list. And as an added bonus, the more you use Q-Notes for other activities, the more confident and natural you will be when you use them to sell better.

PART IV

Face-to-Face

CHAPTER 12

The Sales Conversation— a Relationship in Three Acts

All the world's a stage . . .

—William Shakespeare

Productive Selling is more than just a collection of tools. It's a framework for selling better.

In chapter 2, we talked about the importance of structure when it comes to thinking better and selling better. Whether they are obvious, as in mathematics, or subtle, as in macroeconomics, or sometimes even camouflaged, as in personal relationships, structures help us construct our lives and make sense of the world around us. Structures are everywhere—from soccer games to sales meetings to screenplays.

All the chapters in this book so far have been building up to the heart of the sales process, the sales meeting. It's in the sales meeting (or, in the case of complex transactions, sales meetings, plural) where the real action lies—where the rubber meets the sky, as an old IBM friend used to say.

In the following chapters we will pull apart the sales conversation and show how, at its best, it's a highly structured process, designed to identify, clarify, and open the door to meeting both your needs and those of your clients.

As it turns out, the most useful structure for facilitating commercial transactions owes a lot to the Greek philosopher Aristotle. In 335 BCE, Aristotle observed that the best of Greek drama employed a three-act structure—presenting a story with a beginning, a middle, and an end.

Almost every play you attend, movie you see, or story you hear relies on this same three-act structure—from *A Christmas Carol* to *Toy Story* to *Star Wars*. It's used in novels, comic books, short stories, even video games. The three-act structure builds on the way human beings naturally process complex information. It's as old as mankind's need to communicate.

Act I introduces the characters and their situation, and then presents a turning point, often called a plot point, that forces the protagonist to take some action. This usually takes the first 20 to 30 percent of screen time. Act II throws up challenges to the hero, leading to a make-or-break crisis, which is the second major plot point, and drives the story into the final act. This generally takes up the middle 50 percent of the story. Act III plays out the resolution of the crisis, with the protagonist winning (or losing) the battle. This usually takes up the final 20 to 30 percent of the film.

Star Wars producer Gary Kurtz described how he learned about the three-act structure this way: "I took a master class with Billy Wilder once and he said that in the first act of a story you put your character up in a tree and in the second act you set the tree on fire and then in the third you get him down."*

Here's a graphic representation of the three-act story structure:

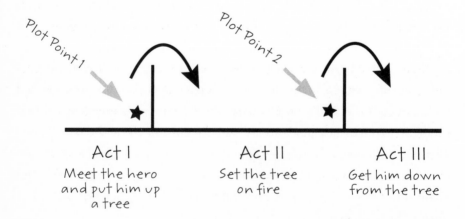

Plot Point 1

Plot Point 2

Act I
Meet the hero
and put him up
a tree

Act II
Set the tree
on fire

Act III
Get him down
from the tree

Los Angeles Times, August 12, 2010. Geoff Boucher, "Did 'Star Wars' become a toy story?" Producer Gary Kurtz looks back.

Like the best films, fairy tales, and fiction, the most productive sales meetings also use a three-act structure—with a beginning, a middle, and an end.

The three acts of the sales conversation are:

I: Earning the Right to Ask
II: Exploration
III: Demonstrating Usefulness

To drive the meeting forward, the first and second acts contain turning points, just as in a drama, that signal the beginning of the next phase of the interaction.

Here's how it works:

In Act I, you work to earn the credibility to ask probing questions. Once you cross the credibility threshold, you propel the meeting into its second act. In an hour-long meeting, Act I may last from ten to fifteen minutes.

In Act II, you explore your client's needs by asking a series of carefully designed questions that help both you and your client better understand the issues and challenges that need to be resolved. Its turning point is the catalytic question—the question that provokes genuine interest, clears away the fog, motivates a desire to act, and opens the door to novel solutions. This turning point drives the meeting into its third act. In an hour-long meeting, Act II may last about thirty minutes.

In Act III, you demonstrate usefulness to your client by offering resources and insights, matching your client's needs to your products or services, and establishing the basis for a continuing relationship. In an hour-long conversation, Act III may last about fifteen minutes (however, if you're really being useful to your client, your meeting may go beyond its original end time).

The chapters in this section of the book, Face-to-Face, go into detail about the three acts of a productive sales meeting, offering tools and strategies to bring them to life.

Chapter 15, The Conversation, Act I—Earn the Right to Ask, discusses eight ways to cross the credibility threshold.

Chapter 16, The Conversation, Act II—Stay in the Question, discusses the art of disciplined curiosity and introduces the concept of reframing through analogies and catalytic questions.

Chapter 18, The Conversation, Act III—Be Useful, shows how you can articulate insights about your client's situation, suggest resources that can help your client, and initiate a transaction.

Here's a graphic representation of the three-act sales meeting structure:

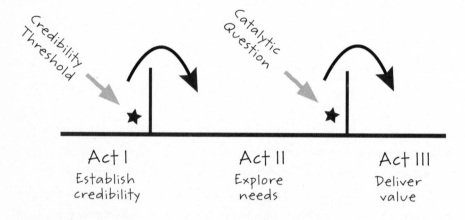

Act I
Establish
credibility

Act II
Explore
needs

Act III
Deliver
value

Like many dramas, the sales story often has a Prologue—an opening scene that takes place before the main story and gives background details that help in understanding things as they unfold. And, like many plays, the sales story may also have an intermission. We'll cover the Prologue to your sales meeting in chapter 14, Prologue—the Meeting Before the Meeting, and we'll discuss how you can derive value from an intermission in chapter 17, Interlude—Give Yourself a Break.

There's one other crucial element in any story or sales meeting—the people involved. Whether in stories or sales, every character has unique interests, traits, hopes, and fears. They take in information in different ways and express themselves in different ways. The better you understand the characters in a story, the more you can appreciate the story itself. Similarly, the better you understand the people in your sales meeting, the more productive you can be. We'll open the door to understanding the characters in your sales meeting in the following chapter.

CHAPTER 13

Cast of Characters—Speak to Be Heard

We don't see things as they are, we see them as we are.

—Anaïs Nin

How is it possible that two people can have a conversation and come away with dramatically different ideas of what was said—who said what to whom and when, the meaning of their words, even the facts and figures that may have been discussed?

Imagine you are listening to your favorite musician performing in concert. Objectively, you hear the same notes, played in the same tempo, as everyone else in the auditorium. One of the songs evokes pleasant feelings for you because it brings to mind a sweet and lovely time in your life. For the woman on your left, the same song evokes pain and longing. For the man on your right, it means something else again. Each of you has a different experience of what, on the surface, appears to be the same thing. And if there are one thousand people in the concert hall, there will be one thousand individual perceptions of that one song.

You may be thinking, "Yes, the emotional response is different, but the music is actually the same. Everyone is hearing the same thing."

But are they?

In trying to unravel how perceptions influence behavior, the American psychologist John Weir suggests the following thought experiment. In the concert hall, imagine that the person on your left is twenty years older than you and has lost the ability to hear high-frequency notes. Does she still hear the same music you hear? Try the experiment on yourself. Listen to some music while cupping your hands over your ears. Do you hear the same music you heard without muffling the sound? What if you add speech to the experience? Is it possible that some words and meanings may be distorted or even missed?

Each of us has a certain acuity of perception. You may have twenty-twenty vision. Or you may need glasses, in which case without them you miss a lot of detail. Weir says that the relative acuity of our sensory receptors—how accurate they are from a purely physiological point of view—is one of a series of filters that influence how we perceive the world.

But Weir's filters go beyond the merely physical.

Let's go back to the concert hall. What if the person sitting next to you is highly trained in music? Would she hear the music in a different way? Would she recognize influences on it—a phrase from Bach in a John Lennon song, for example? Wouldn't her understanding of that influence color her perception of the music?

If we move from music to sports, won't an avid basketball fan see a game quite differently from someone who's never watched one before? Won't a seasoned coach see it differently again? The game is the same, but depending on your knowledge of the sport, you come away with a very different experience of it.

Expertise is one type of filter. Memory of past experiences is another (as in the case of a familiar song). Other filters that influence your perceptions may be gender, mother tongue, ethnic background, economic status, belief system, and the infinite number of other variables that define us.

Because of all these variables, the chance that any two people perceive the same stimuli in exactly the same way is infinitesimally small. If we are all unique, then the different ways we perceive the world are limitless. The bottom line is that you can't communicate with all your clients in exactly the same way and expect them to walk away with exactly the same perceptions of what you discussed.

That's why good communicators—whether they're telling tales or making sales—tailor their words, their gestures, and even the tones of their voices to the people they're talking with—not to be manipulative, but to be effective. After all, if you're having an exchange of ideas, it's helpful if everyone knows what everyone else is talking about.

In order to connect with your clients it helps to understand how they see the world, how they take in information, and how they process it. You have to recognize what gets them moving, what gives them energy—and what saps it. In short, you have to know how they *think* in order to comprehend what they're hearing *and* what they're saying.

You are probably familiar with a variety of personality-typing instruments—short questionnaires that help identify individual thinking styles. If you've ever been employed by a large company, chances are you've taken the Myers-Briggs Type Indicator (MBTI) or some variation of it— such as True Colors, DiSC, the Strength Deployment Inventory, the Winslow personality profile, the Herrmann Brain Dominance Instrument, and many others.

Two of the thinking-style inventories that we've found useful to help understand the dynamics of sales conversations are FourSight, developed by Dr. Gerard Puccio, and NBI, developed by Dr. Kobus Neethling.* Through our experience with FourSight and NBI, we've been able to identify six distinct thinking styles that we've encountered over and over in sales conversations—as well as a set of observable clues in the language they use, the work environments they prefer, the topics that energize them (and those that don't), the way they relate to time, and the way they relate to people.

We'll start with a brief description of the six thinking styles, followed by a set of charts showing common clues that can help you recognize them, and suggestions about the most effective ways to communicate with them—so you can minimize misunderstandings and missed opportunities.

A useful key to communicating effectively is to understand what energizes different people. It's true that our energy changes with our mood, the time of day, our circumstances, and a host of other things, but it's also true that we all have tendencies. Certain things tend to energize us, and certain other things tend to sap our energy. Knowing what energizes (and de-energizes) your conversational partner can make a big difference in the quality of your interaction.

---

*You can learn more about these excellent instruments at foursightonline.com and www.nbiprofile.com.

The six major energizers we've identified are Context, Results, Ideas, Process, Action, and People.

Individuals who are energized by context want to fully understand a situation before they jump into it. They are not comfortable moving ahead until they are clear about possible risks, rewards, or other consequences. They look for measurable criteria to help them evaluate causes and effects.

People who are energized by context enjoy gathering information about issues, trends, and events. They are often skilled at conducting Web searches and may be the first to pull out their smartphones to resolve a discussion with "the facts."

In business, these people ask lots of questions. They may want more detail than others are interested in exploring. They are usually uncomfortable with guesses and unsubstantiated claims. They like the security of understanding what's really going on. People who are energized by context are the folks who make sure the right issues are on the table and the right problems are addressed.

Individuals who are energized by results are interested in outcomes. They focus on the facts, figures, and logic that support their goals. They value communication that is direct and efficient. They are not interested in conversations that go off on tangents.

People energized by results prefer rational approaches, such as cost-benefit analyses, when making decisions. Their decisions and actions "make sense," and they may see feelings as distractions. They measure progress, but they always keep the final goal in mind.

In business, these people are often leaders. They demand precision and accuracy. They don't like ambiguous situations or fuzzy answers. Visions, missions, and targets are paramount for them. At their extreme, they may be ends-justify-means people. People who are energized by results are motivated by setting clear goals and achieving them.

Individuals who are energized by ideas are interested in the big picture. They propose lots of new ideas and imagine possible solutions to problems. They like thought experiments. They get bored by detail and show less interest in the practicalities of bringing solutions into effect.

People energized by ideas enjoy abstract thinking and are comfortable with ambiguity. They see connections between things that others may not. They may respond to rules as suggestions rather than constraints, especially if breaking a rule results in new thinking.

In business, these people can overlook details. In conversations they may bounce around to topics that seem unrelated. They are often playful, irreverent, and independent. People who are energized by ideas are natural creatives. They stretch themselves—and perhaps others—to see new, unexplored, and potentially useful possibilities.

Individuals who are energized by process want to understand how things work. They see the world from a systems perspective. They unpack systems into steps. They like to compare and contrast alternate approaches. They like detailed implementation plans, with timetables and milestones.

People energized by process are careful and detail-oriented. In this way, they are similar to those who are energized by context. Their focus, however, is on systems rather than background. They see the underlying systems in so-called natural behaviors, often identifying opportunities for improvement. They generally have a good grasp of economics, finance, or engineering, and they frequently spot errors and inconsistencies that others miss.

In business, they are neat and organized. They often communicate using matrices and charts. Sometimes their focus on detail impedes their ability to make quick decisions. People who are energized by process are often able to bridge the gap between theory and practice by imposing rigorous, measurable criteria on the projects and people they manage.

Individuals who are energized by action want to see things happen. They are happiest when they are moving toward a goal, even if they aren't completely clear about what that goal is. They are comfortable learning on the job and making course corrections along the way as necessary.

People energized by action are persistent, decisive, and assertive. Once they get an idea, they're already halfway out the door figuring out how to do it. For them, doing is more important than analyzing. They get frustrated if others don't move as quickly as they do.

In business, these people don't shut themselves inside their offices.

They're out talking to others about what's happening and what needs to happen next. They may leap to action before others are ready, and may even appear pushy or reckless. They feel comfortable when they are in control of events. People who are energized by action get things done.

Individuals who are energized by people are gregarious. They see the workplace as a social environment and relate strongly to the people they work with. In evaluating issues, their first concern is how people are affected. They need to "like" proposals before committing to them.

People energized by people are networkers. They have a strong intuitive sense, and usually have a good idea how others will respond to proposals or changes. They want feelings and fairness to play an important role in their decisions.

In business, they may sometimes favor relationship-based decisions over bottom-line decisions. However, because they regularly consult with others, they are also natural consensus builders. If they like an idea, they tend to talk it up within their networks, helping to generate acceptance and recruit support.

You can see these six thinking styles in action in every walk of life. Understanding how others see the world, how they relate to information, and what energizes them can be a useful skill on the job, in your social circles, and even at home. Be cautious, though. We are all a blend of different styles and tendencies. Almost no one works off just one type of energy. We all have our preferences, and recognizing these can be useful, but remember to be flexible. In reality we're all mongrels, not purebred show dogs.

Although there are numerous personality tests that can help identify what energizes people, it's unlikely you'll have the opportunity to sit your clients down in front of a questionnaire or have the time to analyze their results before your meeting. Fortunately, there is another excellent way to identify what energizes people. You can simply observe them. As you'll see below, most of the clues aren't hard to spot.

PEOPLE ENERGIZED BY CONTEXT

Workspace clues Desk and office well organized, free of clutter. Reference books, framed credentials, certificates, mission statements. Few personal mementos. Documents neatly stacked and flagged with Post-its.

Communication clues Analytic, detailed, professional jargon, short forms. E-mails brief, often containing questions. Voice mails crisp, precise. May correct others' inaccuracies or misuse of words. Tend to ask many clarifying and informational questions.

Miscellaneous clues Clothing neat, well thought out, but not stylish or flamboyant. In meetings, may return to issues you think have been fully covered. Are not prepared to make decisions, or even move to the next agenda item, until comfortable that all the facts have been considered.

Connecting

- Expect to cover less ground in your meeting than with other clients, but expect to cover it more thoroughly.
- Begin with an agenda, possibly printed, with outcomes for each item. Stick to it as much as possible.
- Offer detailed, factual support information. Have fact sheets, spec sheets, timetables, price lists, testimonials available.
- When presenting data, make sure that it's accurate and that sources are cited properly. Be prepared to explain and support methodologies used to gather, validate, and interpret data.
- Show how risks are minimized. Highlight contingency plans for the unexpected.
- Be prepared to answer questions about history, sources, data. If you don't know, be frank and offer to find out as soon as possible. Take careful notes on followup information you will need to supply.
- Confirm they are satisfied with each agenda item before moving on. If you jump to giving advice before they think you fully understand their situation, they may view you as shallow or cavalier. A useful question to ask periodically is "Is this enough detail to be useful to you?"
- Don't expect final decisions during the meeting. They need time to think things through. Offer to provide further information in a followup meeting.

PEOPLE ENERGIZED BY RESULTS

Workspace clues	Desk neat and sparse. Little overt evidence of work. Diplomas and formal acknowledgments of achievement on display, possibly a few research reports or executive summaries. Few personal mementos.
Communication clues	Confident, to the point, direct, rational, few niceties. Voice mail often recorded by assistants. E-mails may be sent by assistants, specifying topics, outcomes, start/end times.
Miscellaneous clues	Clothing very deliberate. They are often keenly aware of messages they send through attire, body language, position in room, words used. Often have a strong sense of time and don't want it wasted. They are usually explicit about their concern for the big picture and results. May arrange meetings so they are backlit.

Connecting

- Have an agenda, in headline format, showing clear objectives for each stage of the meeting, but expect them to jump ahead, to what they consider most important.
- Always have an answer to the question "Why are we here?"
- Respect their time.
- Focus discussion on strategies more than tactics.
- Offer logical reasoning. Deliver top-line information, crisply and to the point.
- Be prepared with supporting facts, figures, charts, technical accuracy. Cite authorities, scientific proof.
- Offer frank situation analyses, and be clear about both pluses and minuses of any situation or suggestion. Be candid about costs, benefits, and risks.
- Link your proposal to their success, industry drivers, and strategies. When discussing strategies, always link to results. When discussing results, always be able to offer strategies for achieving them.
- Demonstrate that meeting with you has been a wise and efficient use of their time by being efficient, direct, and results-focused.

PEOPLE ENERGIZED BY IDEAS

Workspace clues   Work area visually stimulating. Reminder notes, photos, articles in evidence. "Creative clutter," stacks of paper, files, desk toys, books, games, and other items that may appear unrelated to work. Desk may not be used at all, other than as a surface to put things.

Communication clues Open, expressive. "Wow!" What if?" "What else?" Conversation meanders or jumps from topic to topic. Use of analogies, metaphors, stories. E-mails written with speed, often containing typos and other errors. Exclamation marks!

Miscellaneous clues Clothing ranges from deliberate and colorful to careless, but almost never conservative. Look for expressions of the big picture. Monitor their energy. They are energized by high-level, abstract thinking. They are de-energized by data, details, and tactics. They may lose track of time as they explore options and alternatives.

Connecting

- Don't offer an agenda. Instead, give them the big picture of the meeting, if possible in visual or metaphoric terms.
- Focus on high-level strategies. Avoid discussing details, tactics, practicalities.
- Use visual imagery, analogies, metaphors, variety, new concepts, future implications. If possible, emphasize the aesthetic qualities of your proposal, its elegance or uniqueness.
- Use pictures, diagrams, back-of-napkin sketches. If possible, float unexpected ideas based on random associations.
- Offer them options, and listen carefully to the options and variants they propose.
- Be prepared for them to jump into brainstorming mode, coming up with many diverse ideas.
- Don't try to rein them in before they are ready. They may feel you're trying to cut them off.
- Respect their intuitive reasoning. Let them riff on assumptions, associations, and ideas. Note these down, even the most unusual ones. Often the unexpected connections they make open new avenues for creative solutions to problems.
- Provide sufficient time for them to incubate ideas. Often this may entail following up by voice or e-mail to give them an opportunity to check, confirm, clarify, or even discard their earlier thinking (you may be tempted to try this during the meeting, but in so doing you may risk undermining the energy of the moment for them).

PEOPLE ENERGIZED BY PROCESS

Workspace clues   Desk clean, functional. Name plates, business card caddies. Process diagrams, flow charts, spreadsheets on walls. Color-coded stacks of paper, laid out in neat rows. A place for everything and everything in its place. Often sit with back to door, facing computer.

Communication clues Careful, precise, often technical, laced with facts, figures. E-mails direct, with few metaphors or analogies. No exclamation marks or emoticons. They take detailed notes, summarize them well, and are often excellent synthesizers of information.

Miscellaneous clues Clothing neat, but not necessarily stylish. May have pocket protectors or other useful gizmos, such as retractable key chains, phone holsters, etc.

Connecting

- Offer a detailed, logical, written agenda. Follow it, refer to it during the meeting, and explicitly confirm if they are ready to move on to the next point.
- Have primary and backup data available in print.
- Use careful and precise language. Provide direct, detailed answers to questions.
- Offer concrete, measurable success criteria.
- Demonstrate the integrity and track record of any process or system you propose.
- Give them a chance to weigh and compare plans and proposals. Leave plenty of time in the meeting for them to ask questions.
- Honor their need to look under the hood and analyze products, services, proposals to see if something will work. Make it easy for them to break down your processes, examine them, and put them back together.
- Offer implementation plans and timetables, including what actions are required at what points and who will be responsible for them.
- Show backup plans and risk-mitigation strategies.

PEOPLE ENERGIZED BY ACTION

Workspace clues   Signs of projects on the go, schedules, to-do lists, reminders. Mementos of past achievements. Desk may be cluttered with recent mess (in contrast to ideas people, whose clutter is often historical). May prefer to meet away from their desk, at a meeting table or living room arrangement. Meeting may be interrupted by calls, pings, brief visits.

Communication clues   Decisive, confident. E-mails characterized by short sentences, e.g., "Saw this, thought u'd be interested." Language shows preference for control with phrases like "What are the next steps?" "Who's on that?" "By when?"

Miscellaneous clues   Because they seek safety by exercising control over situations, they may micromanage. They often want speed, looking for early indications of progress. They are generally comfortable accepting a degree of risk, but are uncomfortable if they don't get feedback on how projects are going.

Connecting

- Honor their need to get going. Avoid long-winded explanations, background discussions, detailed agendas. Instead, use a short-form meeting to-do list, visibly checking things off as you go.
- Stress tactics over strategies.
- When they ask for evidence supporting your proposal, help them visualize how it might work in their situation, what they might learn from experiences of others, and how they might adapt for their own needs.
- Address their need for decisiveness by showing your own. Show that things can move forward quickly, that they will have control, and that they will see near-term progress.
- For these people, no news is bad news, so stress availability of feedback and regular check-ins.
- They don't like missed dates, deadlines, and blown delivery schedules—and they will remember them. Demonstrate that you and your team will respond quickly to their concerns and that you are willing and able to make course corrections along the way.
- They are happy for meetings to end once they feel they have enough information to move on. They always have other things to do, so don't overstay your welcome.

PEOPLE ENERGIZED BY PEOPLE

Workspace clues   Family photos, often of kids at different ages, photos of friends and colleagues, often group shots. Candies, sweets, or other favors on desks. May prefer meeting at a small table, in the cafeteria, or walking down the hall.

Communication clues Friendly. Overt facial expressions. Open body language. E-mails employ exclamation marks, all caps, emoticons. Voice messages may be humorous, or make personal references. In meetings they make the time for climate setting before getting down to business.

Miscellaneous clues May seem to leap out of their chair to greet you. Often welcome you into their space with gestures and a hand on your shoulder or back. Look for signs of informality, references to other people, personal touches.

Connecting

- Avoid pulling out your agenda as soon as you sit down. Warm up first with small talk.
- Have your agenda and planning documents available as backup, but recognize that your client will more likely be comforted by knowing you have them than by discussing them in detail.
- Comment or ask about what you see around you in the office. Try to discover your client's personal interests.
- Use friendly, informal language, expressive words and phrases. Think about what your body language and facial expressions are communicating.
- If possible and relevant, refer to mutual acquaintances or history.
- Expect your meeting to be interrupted by colleagues or staff popping their heads in. Don't be surprised if your client introduces you to them.
- Human interaction is more important to them than logistics or critical paths. Don't burden them with technical or financial intricacies. They prefer to make decisions intuitively, based on emotional input, fairness, empathy, group norms, and opportunities for interpersonal engagement.
- Explain how your proposal will affect the people they work with.
- Offer testimonials and opinions of people they admire and respect.
- Offer opportunities to talk with others who have used your product or service.

The premise of this book is that salespeople are in a unique position to help their clients solve problems. In the end, the more skilled you are in identifying what's important to your clients and how they take in information, the more accurately you'll be able to diagnose their problems and offer solutions that meet their needs.

This energizer model can also give you some clues about your own thinking styles. Are you energized mostly by context, results, ideas, process, action, people, or a combination of two or more? Most of us have more than a single dominant preference. Just because you're primarily energized by people doesn't mean you can't also get energized by ideas. And a person who is primarily energized by results may also have the "go-go" characteristics of someone energized by action. People come in all shapes, sizes, and combinations. You'll need to be sharp-eyed, flexible, and patient to get proficient at identifying these energizers. You'll also need practice. But if you work at it, you'll find that knowing your own thinking styles and getting a sense of your clients' thinking styles will make you a more useful salesperson—able to offer information in a way people can relate to, so they can decide how best to move forward.

Remember too that every strength comes with a flip side, a shadow weakness. By identifying what energizes your clients, you can also begin to identify what they may be overlooking. You can help them consider pieces of the puzzle they may have missed. For example, wearing your context hat, you might help a person who tends to focus on ideas take the time to identify the right problem. Or, wearing a people hat, you might help a person who tends to focus on results consider how a new initiative will affect employees. Or, wearing your process hat, you might help a person who tends to focus on action see that a plan needs more work before going out the door. Often you can demonstrate your usefulness simply by offering new perspectives.

In the end, understanding these thinking preferences and using them wisely is a way of applying a new version of the Golden Rule. As our good friend Ken Wall once said, "It's not do as you would be done by, but do as *they* would be done by, that counts."

CHAPTER 14

The Conversation, Prologue—
the Meeting Before the Meeting

You had me at hello.

—Dorothy (Renée Zellweger) to Jerry (Tom Cruise) in *Jerry Maguire*

Virgil was coaching Steve on his upcoming meeting with Axel. "Okay, so your prep is as prepped as it can be. You've got a handle on the client and his challenges, you're there because of a good referral, you know your scripts, you have some ideas about how you can help. What's the first thing you do in the meeting?"

"Well, I thought I'd lead with my capabilities script and get out the . . ."

Virgil interrupts. "No, before that."

"Before? Oh, well, of course. I introduce myself . . ."

"No, before *that*."

"Before *that*? I don't get you."

"Your meeting doesn't start when you sit down to talk. It doesn't even start with hello. It starts the minute you walk into the building—the minute you even see the building. So what's the first thing you do?"

We've said it several times: the most important moment in the sales process is the sales meeting. And that's true. But that doesn't mean the meeting begins with the formal introductions. Just as in any human interaction, there's usually a prelude to a meaningful conversation.

In a personal relationship, place—the *where* of a get-together—can be part of the prelude, setting the tone of your conversation. You'll have a very different energy level, and a very different kind of conversation, if you meet a friend at a sports bar as opposed to an office or a church social. Place matters.

Another form of prelude is the small talk that almost always precedes the heart of a conversation. Those seemingly inconsequential words about the weather or the traffic or the latest doings of your mutual friends are important. They set the stage for the rest of your time together. They give you clues about how the parties involved are feeling and what might energize them. Like place, small talk counts.

The same holds true in sales conversations. Both place and small talk can have an impact on how successful your meeting will be. So it makes sense to pay attention and be deliberate about how you handle them.

In this chapter we'll discuss two critical sales skills that come into play before the core of the meeting even starts: Becoming a Waiting Room Jedi (how to pick up useful clues from your client's work environment) and Making Small Talk Big (how to reveal the common ground that can turn a meeting into the beginning of a relationship).

You still have a lot of work to do before hello.

Become a Waiting Room Jedi

Sam, an associate of Jane's, was describing a recent experience. "They kept me waiting an hour in reception. What a waste."

"What'd you do?"

"Answered some e-mails, checked my news feed."

"What'd you see?"

"In reception? Nothing. Bad art."

"What'd you hear?"

"Muzak?"

"Did you get the receptionist's name?"

Sam was blank. Jane, as ever, was unrelenting. "What did you think of the men's room?"

"I beg your pardon?"

Jane was tempted to spell out *men's room* for him. Instead, she said, "Look, Sam, last time I had to wait, I asked for the restroom, and where I could get a drink of water. There was a staff kitchen where I introduced myself to a woman getting coffee. Turns out she's the CFO. I told her I was there to see Jay and that I'd put together the Lebowski deal. She says, 'Lebowski, really? Give Jay the details. I'd be interested.'"

"All that because you had an hour to kill?"

"I didn't kill my hour. But it sounds like you did."

Your clients' offices—including reception and common areas—are their habitats. They're filled with clues about the company and its culture. Think of the waiting room as a research opportunity, where you're exposed to resources that aren't available in company reports or on the Web. You can honor the time you and your client will be spending together by being an anthropologist—looking for clues to better understand the people you'll be meeting with. Once you're in your client's territory, the only wasted moments are the ones you decide to waste.

The Well-Traveled Road Phenomenon

Imagine walking down a familiar road. You know it by heart. It's as if your feet take you where you need to go.

Now imagine walking down a road you've never traveled before. You walk the same distance and at the same pace as you did on the well-traveled road.

Which journey seems to take longer? Think about the last time you drove to a new place for the first time. Now think about your return drive home. Which felt longer?

Researchers had people walk on well-traveled and never-traveled roads. Subjects were then asked to estimate the time they spent on each journey. Nearly everyone estimated they spent *more* time walking the unfamiliar road. The researchers theorized that in an unfamiliar environment, we pay more attention. We notice more, and we remember more. The effect is that it *seems* as though more time has passed.*

You can use this phenomenon to your advantage. If it's natural to notice more in a new environment, why not benefit from your heightened awareness? Observe and listen.

There are almost certainly people in the office who know your client, and any interaction you have in the building may yield information and perspectives that can enhance your knowledge, hone your questions, or open up new areas to explore. Based on what you observe, you may be able to add to the questions you've already decided to ask in your meeting. Note these in your Q-Notes.

So if you find yourself with waiting-room time, think of it as a plus. Don't bury your head in your meeting planning notes. You already know the plan. Look for opportunities to make it better—by becoming a Waiting Room Jedi.

Be Curious

The more curious you are, the more you'll learn. It's a simple equation. It's a virtuous cycle.

Stare at the walls. Seriously. That picture of the CEO at a recent ribbon cutting, the artwork, the framed mission and values poster—these are clues. You can learn a lot about the culture your clients work in, initiatives the company is proud of, information on the building you're meeting in, company history, even information about the people you'll be meeting.

Ask questions about everything you see. Say hello to people you run into. Introduce yourself, and tell them why you're there. Or just ask where the restroom is. There's no standard list of things to discover in the waiting room. It's about having your curiosity turned on to whatever you are exposed to.

---

*L. G. Allan, "The Perception of Time," *Perception & Psychophysics* 26 (1979): 340–54; and B. Zakay and R. A. Block, "Prospective and Retrospective Duration Judgments: An Executive-Control Perspective," *Acta Neurobiologiae Experimentalis* 64 (2004): 319–28.

Think about Jane's coffee-room conversation with the CFO. She offered a piece of information (the Lebowski deal), then went where the conversation took her. In doing so, Jane seeded her conversation with her client. "She'd like me to fill you in on the Lebowski deal so you can give her your opinion." Simply by being curious and open, Jane nailed down an important topic for the meeting, met the CFO, and probably established enough credibility with that one exchange to start asking Jay meaningful questions right away. That's the power of being a Waiting Room Jedi.

> There may be reasons to meet at a neutral location: it may save travel time, be less formal, or reduce distractions for your client. However, unless there's a reason not to, we prefer to meet in a client's office. Other than their home, it's the best place to gather personal information about a client. The gym bag on the floor, the framed diploma, the picture of the family at the top of a mountain, the file cabinet covered in piles of dog-eared paper—each of these is information, each of these is a conversation starter. Even if you end up meeting in a conference room, ask to see your client's workspace as part of a tour.

The Receptionist

Receptionists sit there all day. They see all the comings and goings, and usually know everyone in the company. They know way more about the social dynamics and the people in the organization than you ever will, and maybe more than most other employees. Best of all, receptionists are often happy to chat.

Here's Jane arriving for a client meeting at Boston Sabre. Let's see how she practices her Waiting Room Jedi skills.

"Hello, I'm Jane Anders. Here to see Juan. You're Mary?"

"Yes, hi."

"Juan told me I'd recognize you by your smile. Nice to meet you."

"Likewise. . . . Oh, it looks like he's still on a call. I'll check back in a few minutes. You can have a seat. Can I get you anything?"

Jane said, "No, I'm fine," and sat down to wait.

The hell she did.

Why make this the end of their interaction? Instead, Jane initiated a conversation. "I noticed the health club downstairs. Do a lot of people here use it?"

"We get a special rate for being in the building. So it's a good deal."

"Oh, has Boston Sabre been in here a long time?"

"Three years. As soon as we moved in, the health club offered us the discount. A lot of people joined."

"Makes sense. Why'd you move?"

"The company? It was part of a reorganization where they separated corporate from manufacturing."

Jane has a new piece of information about Boston Sabre. "Sounds like there's been some growth."

"You could say! We're already looking for more space."

Jane wanted to know more about the corporate culture. "Are there a lot of active people here?"

"You could say that too! We have company volleyball, basketball, *and* softball teams. It's a young company, and we're a pretty social place. The teams are a good way to burn off stress."

Jane knew about stress. "You bet. . . . Do René or Juan play?"

"See that photo in the case. Juan's the one getting the high fives. That was just after he hit the game winner for the league championship."

Jane could see the energy in Juan's face. "Looks like he likes to win."

"You could say!"

In just a few minutes of friendly interaction, Jane was able to gather several business and personal conversation starters. What might she start to surmise about the things that energize Juan? And what are the chances she'll mention the photograph in her conversation with him?

Of course, she could have spent the time checking her e-mail. But then she wouldn't be Jane.

To transform your inevitable waiting time into productive time, make it a practice whenever you enter a client's territory to introduce yourself, initiate interaction, and look for opportunities to gather data in one or more of the following areas.

- Company history and logistics. Understanding the landscape of the organization gives you context and conversational nuggets for your sales meeting.
- Organizational culture. If the waiting area gives you a view of parts of the office, you can notice how people are working. How do they dress? How do they greet one another? Do you notice camaraderie? Is the place quiet or energetic? Do they bounce problems around? Is the group international, culturally mixed, homogeneous? Noting clues about cultural norms can help in other ways too. For example, language that works well in one environment might be unacceptable in another.
- Ways to link your client to the lobby. What you uncover in the waiting area can be a springboard for conversations with the people you'll be meeting. If a visitor showed up in your office and said, "I heard you just returned from a three-week safari in Kenya," wouldn't you want to talk about it?

Waiting Room Jedi Questions

Make a list of seven questions that you can work into any conversation with the receptionist or any employees you run into in the waiting room. The more your list reflects your personal style and interests, the more genuine and useful it will be. Here are some typical questions to get you started.

- How long has the company been at this location? What prompted the move?
- How many people work here? Who's housed in this building?
- What's the biggest department or division at this location?
- Is everyone always this (relaxed, friendly, energized) around here? Or is there something special going on today?
- What do you like best about working here?
- Are the principals usually around or mostly on the road? Are they engaged in the day-to-day? Do they know everyone in the office by name?

> Often you'll go to meetings with a colleague or two. In the waiting room, you'll be tempted to chat with one another. But how much value will you get from recapping last night's hockey game?
>
> Do the reverse. Take advantage of your numbers. While one of you asks someone passing through about the trophy on display, another visits the restroom, and the third talks to the receptionist. The more you ask, the more you'll learn. Curiosity pays off.

Put on your anthropologist's hat the moment you step into your client's space. If you discover ten pieces of information, a couple of them are sure to come in handy in your conversation.

Make Small Talk Big

Small talk, the informal ritualistic chat that people engage in with new acquaintances, is usually about the weather, sports, traffic, or some other current event. But small talk isn't just throw-away chatter. It lubricates relationships and prepares the way for deeper conversations.

One of the main social purposes of small talk is to overcome the stranger's dilemma that we discussed in chapter 2. No productive human interaction can occur without some level of trust. Whether we're exchanging money for a soft drink at the corner store, agreeing to meet a colleague at a certain time and place, or conducting a major business negotiation, we need to trust that the other parties will live up to their end of the deal—explicit or implicit.

Small talk helps us overcome the stranger's dilemma because it's a way of establishing common ground. If we can discover common ground—shared interests, experiences, or acquaintances—then we become somewhat less strange to each other. It's what you do when you socialize with new people at a party, or chat with your seatmate on a plane. As soon as you discover common ground, your conversation shifts to a new level. You have something to talk about, something the other person can relate to. Even though you've only just met, you've learned a little about the other person, and you begin to feel connected. It's almost like magic. One moment you're a stranger, the next you're on the road to a possible relationship—not guaranteed, but possible.

Think of any business meeting you've ever had with someone you didn't know well. It's almost a guarantee that it started with some form of small talk. It's just the way we human beings work. We ease into conversations.

In business meetings, there are three levels of common ground you can discover through small talk:

- Shared Interest, the most basic level. Your client reveals a personal interest that you are genuinely curious about.
- Shared Connection, a somewhat stronger level. You and your client have shared similar experiences or have loose social connections.
- Shared Community, the strongest level. You and your client are members of a defined community with identifiable culture and values. For example, you're both Rotarians.

In each case, you can look for common ground by asking about the other person and disclosing things about yourself. Here's how Jane used those skills to reveal a shared interest.

Juan's colleague René picked her up in the waiting area. After they introduced themselves, Jane asked, "I saw Juan's high-five picture in the trophy case. Do you play on any of the company teams?"

"A little basketball. I played in college, but I have to watch my knees now."

"Where did you go to school?"

"North Carolina."

Jane's natural curiosity led her to a possible connection worth exploring. "My daughter plays basketball. She talks about playing in the ACC one day."

"It's a tough conference."

"She's undersized but tenacious, a bit like her mom. I only played high school ball. But we made the state tournament my senior year. We played our second round in UNC's facility. I still remember how amazing it felt to look up at the stands from the court. Talk about nervous!"

Jane's disclosure has given something for René to be curious about. "You grew up in North Carolina?"

"We moved there when I was sixteen."

"How did you do in the tournament?"

"Not bad, but not good enough. It was a great experience, though. . . . Did you like NC?"

By being curious and asking questions based on what she had learned in the waiting room, Jane discovered two small areas of shared interest—college basketball and the Atlantic Coast Conference. She and René will likely continue following those conversational threads as they walk to Juan's office.

You can use the same approach to find even deeper levels of common ground—shared connection. Imagine the following scenario:

As part of a handoff, your boss introduces you to one of his clients, David. You start discussing that it might be useful to tour David's plant, and you mention that next week is blocked because you'll be going on your annual vacation to the Michigan Lakes district. David says, "You're kidding. I used to go there every summer for years." A five-minute conversation breaks out about this golf course, that old hotel, and those quaint little towns. In no time, you and David have discovered common ground based on spending your summers in the Michigan Lakes—all because you revealed something about yourself.

The strongest level of common ground is shared community. Again, asking and disclosing are the keys.

Imagine discovering at the beginning of a meeting that you and your client went to the same school or grew up in the same neighborhood. You never met, but you know the same places, the same families, the same history. You even have some mutual friends. The entire tone of your conversation changes with these discoveries. Some people might say, "Man, that was pretty lucky, finding out you grew up in the same town." Others, like Wayne Gretzky, might say, "You miss every shot you don't take." Connections don't usually appear out of nowhere. They appear because you look for them.

One of the reasons shared community is so powerful is that it goes beyond simply *knowing* things in common. Shared community evokes shared *feelings*. If that seems trivial to you, ask yourself this: Who are you more likely to be open to at the beginning of a meeting, someone you have no connection with or someone you share history with? Who are you more likely to trust—to like?

Shared community creates a kind of unspoken loyalty. It's natural for community members to treat one another decently, to give one another the benefit of the doubt. Think of the last time you were traveling abroad and bumped into someone from your home country. Wasn't there an immediate connection? Didn't you both assume the best about each other, at least at first?

Shared interest, shared connection, and shared community may also provide reasons to follow up and check in with your clients—opportunities to remain in their headspace (we discuss this notion in more detail in chapter 20). If you and your client started talking about golf and he mentioned he'd been losing a lot of balls in the rough while working on his new swing, you might think of sending him a box of orange golf balls next spring, accompanied by a friendly note—a typical followup opportunity, based entirely on small talk.

Small talk is an art. Some people are just naturally good at it. But it's also a skill, and, as with any skill, you can improve with practice. Since small talk will happen whether you want it to or not, you might as well get good at it. Here are some ways you can hone your skills:

- Develop the habit of disclosing and asking. Don't just say, "Next week's blocked. I'm going on vacation." Say, "Next week's blocked. I'm going to my favorite vacation spot, the Michigan Lakes district." That gives something for the other person to attach to. Granted, chances are small they'll be familiar with your favorite summer haunt. But they're a lot bigger than if you don't mention it at all. If your client says to you, "We're going on vacation," be interested; ask, "Oh, where do you go?" You never know what you'll discover.

- Start right away—as soon as you greet your client. Ask about something you saw in the lobby, the company's charities, or the awards on the wall. If the office seems unusually busy, ask why. These questions are light, appropriate, and potentially informative.

- Tune in to what your client is offering. Before you get down to business, look at the walls, the desk, the bookshelves, the awards, the golf clubs, the project board, the family photos. People surround themselves with what interests them. They won't mind you asking. Far from it. They'll probably be delighted to talk about them if you open the door. Remember too that the more attention you pay to your client's space, the more likely you'll be able to identify what animates them, and the better you'll be able to communicate with them in a way they can relate to.

- Remember that the things that interest you might also interest others. Let them know about your hike up that fourteen-thousand-foot Colorado peak, your collection of weird South American spiders, or the Thai cooking class you're taking. Every disclosure is a potential conversation starter.

Asking and disclosing is a natural part of almost any social conversation. And there's no reason it shouldn't be part of almost every sales conversation as well. Sharing personal information sends a message: "I'm not just a business drone. I'm a unique human being with a life outside these four walls. I'm interested in who you are, and I'd like you to be interested in who I am. I don't want us to be strangers."

Every time you ask or disclose, you're inviting the other person into a possible conversation. Every time you ask or disclose, you're laying out a sort of magnetic thread. If the thread attracts your client, there's a possibility of a conversation. If not, you can start a new thread by asking another question or disclosing something else about yourself, until you find an area of common interest.

A Special Case for Small Talk—Introducing Your Colleagues

Many people find it uncomfortable to reveal things about themselves out of the blue. One of the advantages of going to meetings with colleagues is that you can do this for each other.*

As he develops business, Matt often takes his boss to crucial meetings— and introduces him like this: "John is the chief of our team. He's also an avid rock climber, which means he's a detail guy. His climbing buddies tell me they appreciate that when he's leading them up an eight-hundred-foot wall."

This simple introduction does three things: it reveals something interesting about John, it highlights his attention to detail, and it offers a conversation thread that Matt's client just might pick up. "No kidding? The other day someone sent me a link of shots of people pitching sleeping platforms

---

*There are lots of good reasons to bring a colleague to your sales meeting. Two brains are almost always better than one. While one of you talks or questions, the other can observe and take notes. Your colleague may add a novel perspective to the discussion. And when you do your after-meeting debrief (chapters 20 and 21), your colleague will remember things about the meeting that you don't. We love working as a team and recommend it.

hanging off thousand-foot walls. I'm thinking, really? Me, the most dangerous thing I do is coach my kid's soccer team. Though between adolescent girls and their parents, hanging off a cliff might be preferable."

"I know what you mean. I coach my kid's team too. We have parents from the Godzilla charm school. Let me know if you have any tips."

Matt's introduction opened the door to a possible question, a story about climbing, or an observation about discipline. As it turned out, John and the client discovered a possible reason to stay in touch. Sometimes there may be no compelling business reason to check in. But if you're both coaching kids' soccer teams, you can send an e-mail after your first game.

To: Client
From: John
Re: Season Opener

Opened our season yesterday. Lost 4–3 in a real nail biter. My daughter Molly scored to tie with six minutes left.
You guys begin yet?
Best luck!

John

PS Matt and I will contact you in June on the line expansion we discussed last month.

Moving into the Meeting

Small talk doesn't have to be long. Investing as little as two or three minutes to find common ground can make a world of difference. But you don't want to overstay your small talk welcome. Take your cue from the client to determine when it's appropriate to move on. A glance at a watch, a terse response to a small talk question, an abrupt change in posture—all these can mean the client is ready to get down to business. And after all, that's what you're there for. There will be chances to return to small talk, but for now, it's time to move on.*

Over the years, Matt has learned how to segue into the business part of a meeting without even rippling the water, like this:

"Have you managed to weather this heat wave?"

"I was lucky. I missed it. We just returned from a week in Maine. It was still hot, but we were right on the ocean, so cooling off was easy."

"Has the weather hit your business at all?"

"The biggest thing is our server farm. Keeping the servers cool is always big bucks, but in this heat it's brutal—two times the kilowatt-hours per day."

"I never really got kilowatt-hours, but doubling anything seems like a lot. Do you have a technical background?"

"I did EE at university and worked as an engineer for years."

"How did you make the move to management?"

"What I liked most about engineering was solving problems. But at my level, it was more kludging patches than finding really innovative solutions. I moved to R&D where there was more flexibility, but after a couple of years, I felt like I was bumping up against the same walls. I finally got that it's the business guys who define the innovation targets. I figured that's where I needed to be, so I got an executive MBA, took on some critical projects, got noticed. So here I am. . . . By the way, the kilowatt-hours to cool our servers? You could heat and cool your house for a year on the amount we use on a normal day for just one of our units. It's a lot. We're talking megawatts."

"I'll remember your servers every time I turn on the AC. . . . So do you rely on your tech background often as a senior executive? Do you worry about things your colleagues don't see?"

Matt turned the conversation toward a search for challenges. He moved naturally from small talk about the weather to Act I of the meeting. He also unearthed clues about his client's thinking styles. With a background as an engineer, he's clearly comfortable with process, but based on his story, he's

---

*Often the level of interest clients show in continuing small talk will be a clue to their thinking styles. Clients animated by ideas or people will generally be happy to continue small talk. Those animated by context, results, or process may be happier to move on to business.

more interested in problem solving and innovation. Matt might guess he's energized by both ideas and results.

A s with any skill, your first efforts at small talk may feel awkward, perhaps even mechanical. Remember, the key to authenticity is your genuine curiosity. If your questions and disclosures are truly based on wanting to know, that's what they'll feel like to the other person. If your questions are just part of a spiel, that's what they'll feel like to the other person. Your underlying attitude will always communicate as much, or more, than your words.

Remember too that small talk isn't a game of Ping-Pong—you don't lose by not returning a volley. If you're not interested in a subject but keep asking, you'll sound like a cross-examiner, and chances are your client will smell your inauthenticity. So instead of trying to fake your way through a topic that's of no interest to you, look for another thread. Your kids, their kids, the atmosphere in the office, and, yes, even the traffic and the weather. Any thread can be a conversation starter.

Of course, sometimes even the most interesting and authentic threads won't connect with people. Don't be discouraged if your client doesn't pick up your invitation. You may be meeting a person animated almost exclusively by results or someone whose primary concern is context. Both these people will be happy to get down to business as quickly as possible.

But more often than not, your small talk will do for your sales conversation exactly what it does in millions upon millions of social interactions every day—make it easier for you to ease into the more serious part of your conversation, by making you less of a stranger to your client.

Small talk works. In social settings. On planes and trains. In shopping malls and waiting rooms. And in business meetings around the world. Its dynamic is simple—it's an invitation to share. And its effect can be profound—transforming a stranger into a prospective client and a prospective client into a possible friend.

CHAPTER 15

The Conversation, Act I— Earn the Right to Ask

The two most important assets any salesperson can have are credibility and curiosity. Without either, there's no sale.

—Matt

J ust as in movies and novels, Act I of the sales conversation brings you and your client into the story and sets the stage for events to unfold.

Act I is about crossing the credibility threshold—earning the right to ask questions that uncover your client's needs. Even the most carefully designed questions won't move you forward if your client doesn't trust you enough to answer them. No credibility, no candor. No candor, no unfolding story.

Clients enter the meeting with their own objectives. One of them is often to *dis*qualify the salesperson. For busy managers, identifying you as someone they don't need to talk to again can be a useful outcome.

So before you even start, you have incompatible objectives: you want to build a relationship; your client wants to weed out unproductive uses of their time. Even though your clients probably don't care about your relationship-building concerns, you need to care about their time-saving concerns. You won't get to your goal until you satisfy theirs. You do that by establishing credibility.

Matt offered to take Steve to one of his sales meetings to show him his approach. On the way over, he briefed Steve on what to expect. "I'm thinking there are only one or two things I can offer Jean. We're a side issue for her company—as a result of an acquisition they made last year. She said she's only got thirty minutes. So I'm going to try to get down to business quickly. My guess is she'll never be a big client. But I could be wrong. These are all still assumptions. I'll check my understanding right off the bat."

"How did you get the meeting?"

"A business buddy of mine recommended me. Louis is a good friend and he's also been mentoring Jean. So it's a solid referral. I'm introducing you as my protégé."

They met in a conference room off the reception area. Matt assumed control of the meeting right away. "Jean, Louis has told me about your company's foray into my line of work—and I thought I might be able to help. Can you tell us your overall strategy objectives for the next eighteen months, how this acquisition fits in, how you'd define success for the acquisition, and what you see as the three biggest impediments to that success?"

Jean smiled. "That's a big question."

"That's my job. Is it answerable in thirty minutes?"

"I believe it is."

"Great. Let's take it in chunks. What's Windward's overall strategy, and what's changed with the new acquisition?"

Thirty-three minutes later, standing at the elevators, Steve said, "Wow, you sure got a lot of information in half an hour."

"Twenty-five minutes, really. I spent the last five offering my best ideas."

"Tell me about that start. You hit the ground running with no small talk. You told me it's important to warm people up to questions like that. You were getting pretty deep, you know. You almost sounded like a doctor taking a medical history."

Matt smiled. "Good observation. So why do you tell your doctor things you wouldn't tell a stranger?"

"Because I trust his motives and expertise. He's there to help and probably knows how. Right. I see—credibility and expertise. But which comes first? Expertise? Credibility?"

"Well, for some people, expertise and acumen get you credibility. Expertise is about knowledge. Maybe the things you know that they don't. Or your capacity for analysis. Or product knowledge. The more you know, the more comfortable they feel answering your questions. Other people relate more to integrity. They want to believe you'll do what you say you'll do, that you'll honor their interest, that you're a professional who will give effort on their behalf. If they trust you to do that, they're comfortable answering your questions. Pretty much like the situation with your doc. You want to believe he knows what he's doing and that he's there to help you. Both are important."

"But you didn't do anything to establish either one. You just fired away."

"I asked a cheeky question."

"I doubt that would work for me."

"A little gray hair helps. So what else was in my credibility account?"

"Well, you had a strong recommendation from someone in her community. But you did launch in pretty quickly."

"We only had thirty minutes. Not a lot of time. On top of that, we weren't in her office. Not many clues about her as a person. So I figured I'd just assume credibility and move to my questions."

"Isn't that dangerous?"

"Let's call it a calculated risk. Look, we knew this was a side business for Jean, right? So I guessed she'd be happy to find someone to handle the hassle for her, especially with the referral. I figure if I ask her relevant questions that show my expertise, she might see a fit. She answered everything I asked. She knows what she wants to get done, and she can't do it herself. Seems like diving in was the right call."

Matt not only assumed credibility, he also started the meeting without any small talk. Why? The sterile meeting room had no small talk starters, and time was limited. If Jean had wanted to chat, she would have mentioned Louis. As Matt said, there is no one "right" way to run a meeting. In this case, he put the meeting on "speed dial" based on his instinct and what he wanted to accomplish.

> Our definition of credibility is the level of trust, legitimacy, or perceived value that allows your client to feel comfortable answering your questions. Once you have earned the right to answers, stop talking, and start asking.

Many Paths to Credibility

In the following pages we'll discuss eight ways to cross the credibility threshold. Their relative effectiveness varies according to the formality of the meeting, the social status and energy profiles of the people in the meeting, and the experience level of the salesperson. We'll consider the pros and cons of each of these methods, and we'll offer general observations about each one.

First, let's go into a little more detail about the key variables.

Meeting Formality

In the Western world, it is generally useful to establish an informal, friendly energy for a meeting. However, there are often circumstances beyond your control that tend to create more protocol-driven meetings. Each of the following will nudge a meeting in the direction of formality:

- Takes place in a conference room
- Involves more than one person from each organization
- Involves the boss of somebody in the room
- Participants wear business suits
- Participants aren't well acquainted

Normally, even a meeting with all the above boxes ticked will begin with some small talk. But be prepared for it to shift to a more formal tone.

Social Status

Every human interaction has a status dynamic. Personality, expertise, hierarchy, age, culture, goals, protocol, when and where you meet—all of these, and more, determine the relative status levels of people in a meeting. If you're meeting with the CEO, you'll probably instinctively take the lower-status role. If you're the wizened subject matter guru, people will generally grant you higher status. If you're the one asking for an audience, you probably have lower status. And so on.

The status dynamic is not a judgment about your relative worth. It's just the social role you occupy in a given situation. Nor is status necessarily fixed. Higher and lower levels often shift back and forth depending on what is happening during a meeting.

Thinking Styles and Energy Preferences

In chapter 13 we discussed the characteristics of individuals who are energized by context, results, ideas, process, action, and people. People with different styles will grant credibility according to how they see the world. For example, people energized by results will usually grant credibility to someone with a proven reputation; people energized by context may withhold credibility until they are satisfied that all the groundwork has been done; and people energized by people will want to establish a human connection before they feel comfortable trusting someone.

Experienced or Novice Salesperson

Some pathways to credibility, such as a strong referral, are more readily available to salespeople with long track records. Others, such as cogent industry commentary, may be excellent approaches for people with less sales experience.

L et's see how these key variables—level of formality, relative social sta- tus, thinking style of your client, and your own level of experience— play out in the eight most useful approaches to crossing the credibility threshold.

The first three strategies rely on a sense of shared community to build credibility.

Credibility Crossing #1: A Strong Referral

There's a reason this is first on the list. Referrals from existing clients, or anyone who has credibility in your industry, kill two birds with one stone— they usually get you a yes to your request for a meeting *and* almost instant credibility.

Early in the meeting, your client will often signal if your referral has gotten you across the credibility threshold. "Rachel is a mentor of mine and a visionary in our industry. She's also really smart. If she says you're worth talking to, that's the highest compliment you can get in my book. Thanks for coming by."

This was the scenario we just saw with Matt and Jean. Jean was happy to meet with Matt—and answer his questions—based solely on her mentor's recommendation.

Pros: You begin with a receptive client. You save time. You can move right to questioning.

Cons: You haven't earned the credibility yourself. It was given to you by your referrer. It has also created high expectations. You'll have to be very solid to maintain them. A poorly run meeting will reflect badly on you. (It may reflect badly on your referrer too. If the meeting wasn't good, make sure you let your referrer know, though she'll probably find out anyway.) Good meeting or bad, make sure you thank the person who got it for you.

Observations: Referrals can shortcut the whole front end of the sales process—finding clients, mining your network, building a prior connection between you and your client, and getting a yes to your meeting request. All these are already done if your existing clients or contacts recommend you to new prospects.

Referrals rely on the dynamics of shared community. Most people want to protect their reputations with other community members. So they are careful who they refer to whom—and how often they leverage this privilege. Referrals say, "I vouch for this person."

Credibility Crossing #2: Personal Connection

Through small talk, you discover a personal connection. You went to the same village in Italy for vacation last year and missed each other by only a week. Their brother-in-law is your second cousin. You both practice aikido and spent time at the same dojo. Your small talk has revealed something your prospect does that you share.

Discovering a personal connection is enough for most people to be willing to answer the questions a salesperson asks. We like to do business with people who are like us.

Pros: If your shared community is strong enough to get you credibility, it will also usually offer many touch points—opportunities to follow up and reconnect with your client. It's also an ideal approach for people energized by people.

Cons: Shared community doesn't build business credibility for everyone. Results-oriented people, for example, may want proof of effectiveness. If the office you enter is large, Spartan, and neat, and your client's greeting is "I'm Draco Martinet, managing director of Kaatsen Development. You have thirty minutes," it's probably not useful to assume high or peer status and casually ask about a picture on the wall. Draco probably won't enjoy more than the briefest small talk, and might even signal this by saying "Okay, let's talk about why we're here." So grant the Dracos of the world their high status, and be aware that despite any small talk connections, you have not yet crossed their credibility threshold.

Observations: When you start exploring social connections, you are signaling equal status. But even sociability has its constraints. A senior ana-lyst won't talk about his ski trip to Beaver Creek for very long if the CEO is waiting. Once the meeting proper begins, you may find you have to assume a lower status. Don't expect the CEO's premeeting friendliness to carry through to the business part of the conversation.

Remember too that crossing the credibility threshold is only the first part of the meeting. Your real purpose is to uncover your client's needs. So don't succumb to the temptation to stay in the comfort zone of personal connections too long. Once you've established enough credibility to ask questions, move to Act II of the meeting: start asking and listening. You'll find greater chances of success, particularly if you are a novice, by moving into a low-status, process-leading role and getting down to business.

Credibility Crossing #3: Business Connection

Simply knowing (or sometimes even knowing of) people in the industry is often a useful way of establishing credibility. "You used to work at Pelota. Did you know Mike Bosh?"

"You bet. Mike's the most positive, tough-minded guy I ever worked with. I learned a lot from him, even though we do have very different styles. How do you know Mike?"

The more business connections you have in common—or the more peo-ple you know who your client might like to meet—the more credibility you can establish. Shared community is powerful. Each person's reputation is on the line. You both have a stake in being productive, to increase your store of interpersonal currency within the community. It's the essence of the good ol' boy/gal network.

Pros: The business connection requires little to no preparation. The more you do it, the more stories you hear and people you connect to one another, the easier it is to do. And it can be fun: the relationship tree of who did what with (and to) whom can be a powerful source of conversation and, ultimately, credibility.

Cons: Be judicious about name-dropping. It can appear egotistical to talk about all your high-level contacts.

Observations: Who-you-know is a veteran's game. You have to have been around awhile to build a network of connections.

The next two strategies rely on professionalism and a sense of protocol to establish credibility.

Credibility Crossing #4: Scripting

Use your scripts. Professional speakers know the value of those first few moments in front of an audience. They plan, refine, and rehearse to get them just right. They step onto the platform, shake the emcee's hand, pause at the lectern, thank the venue, and begin speaking in a firm, clear voice. The audience relaxes, confident they are in the hands of a professional.

Your scripts won't be quite as formal as that, but they should provide your client with a cogent summary of who you are, the company you represent, and why you're there. Your scripts should highlight what differentiates you. They should state how or why you can offer value to your client. And they should set the stage for a productive conversation, in which your client is confident she's in the presence of someone who knows what they're doing.

The psychologist Frederick Herzberg coined the term "hygiene factor" to describe the qualities of something that may not make us feel positive about it, but that if absent make us feel negative.* You don't jump up and down for joy if your hotel room sheets are clean, but if they're not, you'll probably want to switch rooms—or hotels. Similarly, good scripts can be a hygiene factor. A well-designed and well-delivered script won't necessarily seal the deal on credibility, but it can help your client feel confident about spending time with you. On the other hand, fumbling along without making a point can easily leave the impression you're incompetent.

Pros: Aside from a little customizing, you won't have to do extra work to

---

*F. Herzberg, "One More Time: How Do You Motivate Employees?" *Harvard Business Review* 46, no. 1 (January–February 1968): 53–62.

create scripts. They should be a standard part of your kit. Scripting is also an excellent approach for a novice. The question that's built into the end of every script is a useful way to check the temperature of your meeting: How ready is your client to answer your questions?

Cons: Scripting may get you only part of the way to credibility. If it's obvious you're reciting a script, your client may also want to see how well you can think on your feet. On the other hand, if your scripts are too smooth (and the more you practice them, the slicker they'll get), you may come across as canned and inauthentic. It's a fine line.

Observations: Don't forget to stop talking. A script should be no more than a minute in length—less, if possible. Deliver your point, followed by a question. Then stop. If you keep rattling on, you'll defeat your purpose. That's the mistake Steve made with Ian earlier in this book. Scripts can be useful to start your meeting, but we call these things sales *conversations* for a reason. You're after credibility, not an Oscar.

Scripts can also convey slightly higher status, since you're stepping into a teaching role. That's one reason it can be so tempting to keep talking. But the longer you talk, the less time you'll have for listening. So after your scripts have done their job, shift the dynamic (and status). Let your client be the teacher.

Credibility Crossing #5: Professional Implementation of the Meeting Process

When the face-to-face interaction begins, make sure that everyone is introduced, and that everyone's role is clearly stated. Take a moment to look each person in the eye and say his or her name. If you're likely to forget names, scribble down the first two letters as soon as you can. If you think this so obvious that it's hardly worth mentioning, think back to a time when a proper introduction didn't happen and what the consequences were.

Taking introductions in hand, especially if they are about to be overlooked, is also a gentle way of asserting a degree of authority and demonstrates process expertise.

Another way to take control of the meeting process is to explain what you'd like to accomplish and how you'd like to accomplish it. Then ask permission. "How much time do we have? Here's what I'd like to accomplish. I'd like to understand in more detail what you do and how you do it, and what hurdles you need to overcome. I'll ask a lot of questions. When it's useful I'll communicate information about me or my organization. And of course, if you have questions or want more detail, ask me at any time. At the end of the meeting I'll share all the connections I made, ideas I have, and ways I think we may be able to help you. Then we can decide if there are any logical next steps. Are you okay with that?"

You have a plan. You have a process. Like a sommelier at a fine restaurant, you're the expert, *and* you're fully in service to your client. You lead the interaction from that position of service.

Another way to control the meeting process is to use a presentation. More formal than a script, a presentation, especially a tailored one that requires research, demonstrates effort. The work you did, the time you spent, the insights you uncovered—all these demonstrate your commitment to being useful. Effort can be a significant credibility builder.

We were working with some investment bankers at Société Générale. In their world, a sales meeting is nearly always a pitch, and usually involves a prepared presentation. "One meeting I had," a banker told us, "we never even got through the first ten slides. They started asking questions. We asked questions about their questions. We thought we were going to a meeting and instead a conversation broke out. It was the best meeting I ever had."

There's a powerful lesson here: the primary purpose of your presentation is *not* to transmit content. Rather, it's to trigger questions—either yours or theirs. Ideally, your client will begin to ask questions about what you're saying. If they don't, watch for reactions to things you say or show. Ask about the reactions you notice. Like a script, every presentation should have questions embedded in it, either in the form of an interjection by you, or simply a slide with a question on it.*

---

*Thanks to Cathy Pharis for this Productive Selling insight.

Pros: Whether you ask for permission to lead the meeting or to use a presentation, you now have control of the meeting. By using a tailored presentation, you can craft what you want to say in advance, make your key points efficiently, and shorten the credibility-building stage of the meeting.

Cons: A poor presentation can erode as much credibility as a good one can build. So make sure your piece is well designed, well rehearsed, well delivered, compelling, and *short.* Presentations carry the same potential risks as scripting. Getting caught up in a monologue, especially a long one, can be a disaster. No one wants to sit through a fifteen-minute history on your revered founder. Even with a well-crafted presentation, people energized by results or action may resist giving up control. Both are likely to react quickly if they think you're wasting their time.

Because of these risks, it's critical that you build question opportunities into your presentation—they can give you (and your client) an escape valve. Before diving into detail, ask: "I sometimes forget to ask people how familiar they are with this stuff, and I'll give too much detail to people who don't need it, or not enough to people who do. How familiar are you with this, so I can calibrate my description so it's most useful to you?"

Observations: Most clients will let you have control if you ask for it. They're happy to let you succeed or fail on your own terms. Asking for process control is a lower-status approach. It's still your client's meeting. They're just ceding control for the moment. If your client grants you control, always follow up with two questions: "How much time do you have?" and "What would make this meeting useful to you?"

Using a presentation is a useful approach for a novice. It takes the focus off you at the beginning, and puts it on the screen. This can be helpful if you're nervous. Your presentation also gives you an overt structure to follow, reducing the chance you'll forget something important. When preparing your presentation, *prepare to be interrupted.* Your goal is *not* to make the presentation, it's to gain credibility, engage the client, and then find ways to be useful.

Your request for process control can appeal to people energized by process, who want to understand how things will proceed, to people energized by context, who appreciate being oriented, and to people energized by results, who are interested in outcomes (though if they think you're heading in the wrong direction they will quickly wrest control back).

What if your client wants to run the meeting? If they have an approach they want to take or territory they want to cover, let them. Your aim is to give them what they need—which will usually be answers to their questions. Once you've done that, chances are you'll have earned credibility. Follow up with, "Glad I could help you get what you needed. Your questions raised a couple of questions for me. Is it okay with you if I explore a few things?"

The next two strategies rely on your content expertise and your reputation to establish credibility.

Credibility Crossing #6: Cogent Industry Commentary

Offering insightful and novel perspectives on current industry trends can be a powerful way to build credibility. We're not talking about simply regurgitating what everyone else is saying. Your insights have to be novel, unique, and indelibly tied to you. To develop these insights, you have to talk to people, read, and think until you have an angle that's your own. To help you define and refine your insight, keep your radar up while doing your research, talking with your colleagues, and engaging with your network.

Our friend Allan Edelson, a salesperson in the mortgage industry, once uncovered the following insight and used it time after time to establish instant credibility with clients. In a low-interest-rate environment, fixed-rate loans amortize faster in the early years of the loan term. Here's how he explained it: In years twenty-eight to thirty of a thirty-year loan, the bulk of each monthly payment goes toward reducing the principal, and very little toward interest. Because the monthly payment is smaller for a 3 percent loan than for an 8 percent loan, the 3 percent loan will pay *less* of the loan balance at the *end* of the term. By definition, then, more principal is paid at the *beginning* of the term. So lenders benefit from "hyper-amortization" in a low-interest-rate environment. Allan's insight established his expertise and novel thinking capacity. It was a great credibility builder.

Pros: Industry insight is a powerful differentiator. You may be able to use a single insight with many different clients.

Cons: Since it's a script, it carries the usual dangers of scripting. Be mindful to move from your role as a professor to your role as a questioner and listener.

Observations: This is a high-status approach. At least for the moment, you're taking the role of a sage. It's also novice-friendly (as a novice you'll question things that industry mavens won't). All it takes is research, smarts, and effort. Once you've done the work, your analysis can have a reasonably long shelf life.

A unique industry insight will usually resonate well with context-, idea-, and results-oriented people because it clarifies industry issues and often offers a big-picture perspective on industry drivers.

Credibility Crossing #7: Your Reputation Got You There

If your name and your work are well known by many people in your industry or niche, your reputation alone can buy you the credibility to move swiftly into Act II of the sales conversation. As a seasoned professional, you can take a high-status role if you choose to.

Pros: It requires no preparation (your whole career has been your preparation), and you can get right to the questions you want to ask.

Cons: Expectations are high. Your client might be looking for reasons to say, "I met that old war horse. He's living in the last decade."

Observations: Having a reputation that gets you meetings is not available to everyone. But it's certainly worth building up to. Some salespeople develop expertise in an industry niche. They get a word-of-mouth reputation in that specific domain, and then begin to leverage their reputations to get meetings in the wider community.

The final strategy—simply assuming the credibility you need—is usually used in conjunction with one or more of the other methods.

Credibility Crossing #8: Assume It

As Matt did with Jean, one way to assume credibility is by asking revealing, strategic questions right off the bat—big, in-your-face gorilla questions, such as, "How has your strategy changed in the last year, and what are the three most important challenges that creates for you?"

Be prepared to endure the silence that's likely to follow. Your client may have to gather his thoughts before answering. If your client decides he's not yet ready to answer, he'll make it clear, by saying something like, "Before I do, I want to understand a bit more about you and your organization." And you'll probably respond with a short script. On the other hand, if your client does begin to answer your gorilla question, you've rolled right into Act II—the exploration part of the meeting.

Pros: It's time-efficient, and can leapfrog you into Act II. It's a surprise. If you want to establish yourself as bold, it's effective.

Cons: You need a backup plan. If your client isn't ready to go that deep that fast, you might fall back on a script that answers the question for your own company. In theory, your firm's strategy should explain why you are sitting in front of this client. That's a useful set of dots to connect.

Observations: Asking the gorilla question is a high-status move. You have declared you are worthy of your client's explanations of their business plans. As such, it usually works best in conjunction with another method, such as a strong referral, or industry reputation.

The gorilla question changes the energy of the meeting abruptly, from chat to exploration. By asking it, you've taken formal control and declared that the meeting is now "officially" starting.

Assuming control in this way isn't a demonstration of expertise so much as a declaration of expertise. By asking the gorilla question, you're asserting you can do something with the answers you'll get. You'll need a lot of confidence and expertise to start the meeting this way.

This approach is likely to work best with ideas-oriented people, who enjoy connecting the dots, and results-oriented people, who like to think in big-picture terms.

———

U ntil you establish sufficient credibility, your client won't be comfortable answering the questions you'll need to ask in Act II. Some clients will grant you credibility right away. Others will need more persuading. It may take two seconds or two years. Your credibility in each instance is likely a combination of the approaches we've discussed in this chapter. The key is figuring out when you have it so you can move to the next stage of your meeting—where you focus on exploring and trying to understand your client's reality.

Once you've crossed the credibility threshold—your turning point—you need to move on, or you risk losing your audience. A client ready for the meat of the conversation won't tolerate your continuing to set the table. It may feel comfortable to chat about mutual acquaintances, but you can't begin exploring your client's needs until you move from chitchat to business talk.

CHAPTER 16

The Conversation, Act II—
Stay in the Question

Asking questions is giving yourself permission to listen.

—Virgil

For several years, we've been conducting an informal brain study in our seminars. In a moment, we'll show you two sentences, one after the other. Your job is to determine which of the two sentences stimulates you to think more.

First, take a moment to clear your mind. Take a breath or two. Expect nothing. Then, once you are relaxed, read the sentence in the box on this page.

Ready? Breathe. Now read the words in the box below.

> **Singapore is far from here.**

Now that you've read the sentence, observe what your mind is doing. See if you can describe to yourself what's going on in your head in reaction to the sentence above.

Then, when you're ready, turn the page to read the second sentence.

How far is Singapore from here?

Again, observe what your mind is doing. See if you can describe to yourself what's going on in your head in reaction to the sentence above.

What happened? Which sentence generated more activity in your brain, the first, the statement, or the second, the question?

In the years we've been conducting this simple experiment, about 75 percent of those surveyed say the question stimulates more brain activity.

"Singapore is far from here" just sits there, perhaps inviting agreement or disagreement. "How far is Singapore from here?" begs a response. Perhaps you reflected on how long the flight might be or how many time zones away it is. Maybe you visualized the map or globe in your head and estimated the mileage. Human beings are question-answering creatures. When we hear a question it's almost as though we can't help but try to answer it—even if the answer is "I don't know." We are uncomfortable with unanswered questions. Our minds naturally look for resolution. It's what we do.

The Power of Questions

Questions are particular ways of articulating problems. If your problem is a shortage of money, you can ask, "How might I earn more money?" or, "How might I budget better?" If you don't have enough free time, a useful way of articulating the problem is, "How might I make more free time?" Your mind immediately looks for answers to questions. You can't help it. You're only human.

We also know there's a universal, three-step process that virtually all humans rely on to respond to questions, puzzles, and problems:

- See the problem.
- Choose a solution.
- Do (or say) something.

Usually this natural strategy works pretty well. From the moment we first climbed out of trees and walked across the African savanna, human beings have used it to avoid danger, find food, and survive hardship. But sometimes it can get us into trouble, especially if two of us are confronting the same problem at the same time (in a sales meeting, for example).

As we've said earlier, one of the main goals of a sales meeting is to uncover a prospective client's problems. Because your aim is to be useful and demonstrate your value, it's natural that as soon as you discover a problem you'll want to offer ideas to solve it. You might say something like, "Here's a suggestion that should help you with that."

But think for a moment. What's the real effect of your statement? Put yourself in your client's shoes. They've likely had this problem for a while. And it's a significant one. Why else would they be talking to people about it? They've been struggling with this problem for months, and after two seconds' thought, some guy they don't even know blurts out, "Try this." How would you feel?

Remember our discussion of the Gator Brain in chapter 2? Not only are you "invading" your client's territory with your solution, but by jumping to a solution so quickly, you're also positioning his problem as simple—a no-brainer. And if the problem he's been working on for months is a no-brainer, what does that make him? Your suggestion is also an aggressive move into a high-status role. Isn't it likely your client will see both you and your "solution" as a threat?

In the natural flow of conversation, the next thing your client's Gator Brain will almost certainly do is resist—either by raising an objection to your brilliant idea (costs too much, not enough manpower, boss won't go for it) or telling you he's already tried it and it didn't work.

Your suggestion leads directly to his objection. Do not pass go. Do not collect two hundred dollars.

But it gets worse.

Once you've proffered your suggestion, you own it. It's your baby. And, like any good gator, *your* first reaction will be to protect it. You threatened your client with an unprovoked idea. Now he threatens you by saying your idea is no good. No one likes to be told their idea is wrong. So your natural instinct is to go on the defensive. (You can just see the two gators, mouths wide open, roaring at each other, can't you?)

Once you and your client, however innocently, have drawn the battle lines, it's going to be difficult to get back to a productive conversation. So the natural flow of the conversation will likely go like this:

Client states problem → You offer idea for solution → Client rejects idea → You defend idea → Client refines objection → You refine defense → Client rerefines and restates objection → You rerefine and restate defense → And so on . . .

Not very productive, is it?

Designing an effective sales conversation means being strategic—and in this case, being strategic means resisting the urge to offer your "solution." To paraphrase Michael Porter, "The essence of strategy is choosing what not to do." (And then not doing it.)*

Stay in the Question

Practice using the stay-in-the-question strategy. Suppress your instinct to blurt out "good" ideas as soon as you get them. Instead, listen to the problem, use your curiosity to help you understand it from the client's perspective, capture your ideas in your Q-Notes, and move on to the next problem.

Here's why.

First, you'll avoid a Gator Brain standoff.

Second, when you give yourself time to incubate an idea, either you'll see why it wasn't so great (or appropriate) in the first place, or it will actually *grow* in power and relevance. In either case, you'll benefit from waiting.

---

*Michael E. Porter, "What Is Strategy?" *Harvard Business Review* (November–December 1996), pp. 61–78. Parenthetical comment by Paul Groncki.

With very few exceptions, you'll be better served (and so will your client) if you deliver your ideas at the *end* of the meeting, when you have the most context and when your client is really ready to hear them. Make it a rule: If you get an idea in the middle of the meeting, jot it down in Quad 2. If, by the end of the meeting, you decide it's still worth communicating, it will have percolated in your ol' thinker and be better tempered when you offer it.

Like any new behavior, waiting to offer your gems will feel unnatural at first, even uncomfortable. But with practice, it will become easier. And with experience, its value will become self-reinforcing.

Here are three Productive Selling tools to help you stay in the question: High Five, Open-Ended Questions, and AIM.

High Five

High Five is a questioning template that helps you and your client get a fuller understanding of your client's situation and challenges. As you'll see, it also positions you as a person who is both willing and able to get to the heart of an issue.

High Five is a "handy" mnemonic—think of the fingers on your hand as four *I*s and the shape made by your thumb and index finger as a *V*. The *I*s are cues for four questions that dig into the challenge: What's the Itch? (in other words, what's irritating about the current situation?), What's the Impact? (what's the effect of the irritation?), What's the Information? (what do we know about the situation and what might we need to know about it?), and Who's Involved? (who's affected by it, who might cause it, who might benefit if it were resolved?). The *V* is a reminder to explore how the issue links to Visions and Values (how significant or central is the issue to the visions and values of the company and the people who work for it?).

Let's peek in on Matt's meeting with Ray, a potential client in light manufacturing. Matt's product is regulated by several government agencies: highway departments need to be notified prior to shipping, and transporting through tunnels is prohibited.

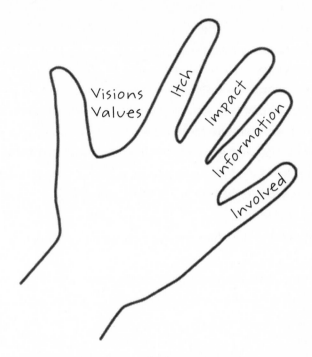

Ray started by expressing an itch. "Last time we did business with a supplier like you, there were three different departments we had to deal with and nine forms to complete every time we scheduled a delivery. It averaged six business days just for the supplier to get a delivery approved."

Matt might not be able to solve the big problem as stated. But by exploring the impact of Ray's itch, he'll have a lot more angles from which to generate ideas.

"Hmm, tell me more. How does that impact business as usual?" *(What's the impact?)*

"Well, part of the reason we do only six-month contracts is that we keep hoping someone will streamline the approvals process. Streamline, and we'd sign up for a year or more. The live signature requirement is a huge hassle. My boss once had a FedEx package chase him around the country, from L.A. to Miami and back to New York. It was nuts."

"So it's the signatures that are the major cause of the delays. What else?" *(What's the information?)*

"The signatures, the number of approval steps. I don't know. Seems to me if we didn't need live signatures, it would save a lot of time. I mean, why not computer signatures? Don't get me wrong, I understand the need for safety. We all do. But if you can transfer millions of dollars without a signature, why not this?" Matt was getting a strong sense of Ray's frustration—and some ideas that might be useful. But he still needed a better handle on the issue.

"Aside from you and your boss, who's involved in those deliveries?" *(Who's involved?)*

"The plant manager in Maryland. She was particularly annoyed."

"What's her role?"

"Well, in the end, she's the one who gets the flak. She and I, I should say. Our line guys lost eight hours on that last delivery. That costs money. But it's more than that. Production line delays bug us all."

"Why?" ("Why?" or "Why is that important?" are useful ways to probe for links to visions or values.)

"Two reasons: money and respect. Obviously, if the line is down we lose money—overtime, wasted resources, opportunity costs. Plus it's disrespectful. Our line people had to work late to meet our commitments. They have families. If they're stuck on the floor, first thing they think is the suits don't care about them. That costs money too. It's tough to quantify, but ticked-off employees extract their pound of flesh somehow, or they leave."

By asking the High Five questions—What's the itch? What's the impact? What's the information? Who's involved? and How do these things relate to the company's visions and values?—Matt gained a fuller understanding of Ray's delivery issues. He uncovered their knock-on effects. And (as we'll see) he was able to identify several opportunities to offer help. Even if Matt doesn't make the sale, Ray is likely to remember this discussion because Matt showed he was willing and able to get to the heart of an important issue.

High Five can help you and your client unpack almost any issue. The process is straightforward:

- Ask your client to articulate one or more itches—those things that bug them, that are out of balance, that create worry.

- Explore the impact of each itch—why is it a problem?
- Probe for more information about the itch—what are its known causes, what *doesn't* the client know about it that might be useful to discover?
- Find out who's involved in the itch—who's affected by it, who might cause it, who might benefit if things were to change?
- Dig deeper to understand how the itch links to the visions or values of the organization or its people.

Open-Ended Questions

High Five illuminates the present situation, its possible causes and its effects. Once you've gotten a good understanding of those, it's time to look forward and begin to explore the future—a future in which your client's itch might be resolved.

It's tempting to offer your ideas right away. But as we said earlier, it's way too soon for that. Remember, at this stage of your sales meeting, *statements are your enemy.* They'll usually do little more than raise resistance. But *questions are your friends*—especially open-ended questions.

Open-ended questions are simply questions that cannot be answered with a yes or no (or a number or a piece of historical data). The most useful open-ended questions usually take the form of "How might we . . . ?" or "How *else* might we . . . ?" Questions posed in this way have many possible answers. They are invitations to think, to speculate, and to discuss.

Let's see how Matt uses a "How might we . . . ?" question to move the meeting along.

As a result of his High Five exploration, Matt has already formulated a basic idea for Ray. Although there's no way around the regulatory process, Ray's company might be able to off-load the hassles around it by subcontracting the approvals process. It's a possible solution, but it's also pretty obvious. Ray might have already looked into it. So instead of making the suggestion, Matt can rephrase it as a question.

But not just any question.

A closed question, such as "Have you thought of hiring a contractor?" won't move the discussion forward. It's really just an idea disguised as a question. Matt needs something broader, something more exploratory. He needs a question that might be answered with the subcontractor idea, but that might stimulate other thinking as well; something like, "How might we leverage other people's expertise to break these logjams?"

The beauty of open-ended "How might we . . . ?" questions is that they stimulate thinking rather than shutting it down. In this case, Ray is likely to offer his views, not as an objection to the suggestion of subcontracting but in answer to Matt's question. "For us it's those three live signatures. People are traveling, on vacation, who knows what? It's ridiculous. I'm thinking preapprovals, or an electronic approval, or allowing scanned signatures. There has to be a better way."

In response to Matt's open-ended "How might we . . . ?" question, Ray has begun to generate his own list of possible solutions. If any of these are feasible to Matt, he will bring them up later. He already knows Ray will be receptive. Matt's company already uses scanned signatures for in-house work, so he jots "SIG. Scan" in the upper-right-hand corner of his Q-Notes.

Matt turned a run-of-the-mill idea into an open-ended question. Had he proposed his subcontractor idea, he might have started circling down the *suggest* → *object* → *defend* drain. Instead, he asked an open-ended question, and Ray opened the door to some possible solutions.

AIM

In our work with clients we also use a questioning technique called AIM to help them dive deeper into their issues. AIM is an efficient way to reveal why your clients need to solve their problems, what the current barriers to solution are, and what other benefits might occur if their problems were solved. AIM is an acronym that stands for Advantages, Impediments, and Maybes. Like High Five, it's simple but powerful.

AIM is particularly useful to help identify the key questions that, if answered well, will deliver real value to your client. We call these catalytic questions, and they are central to the Productive Selling process. We'll discuss them in more detail in a few pages. But for now let's see how you can use AIM to identify them.

Start by looking at the itch. Then ask three simple questions: What are the advantages of resolving this issue? What are the impediments to resolving this issue? What are the maybes (in other words, what else might happen if this issue were resolved)?

Using Ray's company as an example, the itch might be expressed as, "If only we could have on-time deliveries and eliminate administrative hassles."

Matt and Ray would then work together to make a list of reasons this would be good to do—in other words, "What might be the advantages of resolving the itch?" The list they generate might include statements such as:

- We could reduce time and cost of product releases.
- We could reduce overtime costs.
- We could keep our employees happy.
- We could operate at higher efficiency.
- We could be more competitive.

Each of these statements can, in turn, trigger new problem questions, such as, "How might we reduce overtime costs?" or, "How might we keep our employees happy?"

After listing the advantages, move on to the *I* for impediments and ask, "What are the impediments to resolving our itch? What's in the way?" For Ray these might be:

- Too much bureaucracy
- Live signature requirement
- Regulated products
- The density of our compounds, which necessitate regulation

Each of these too can be phrased as a new problem question, such as, "How might we eliminate or reduce bureaucracy?" "How might we eliminate the live signature requirement?" or "How might we reduce our need for high-density compounds?"

Finally, think about the maybes—things that *might* happen if you resolved the various concerns. For Ray, these might include:

- If we kept our employees happier, we might be able to reduce turn-over costs.
- If we used a lower-density compound, we might be able to expand into new markets.

Neither Matt nor Ray knows these things will happen. But they are possibilities. And they could trigger Productive Thinking about the company's future.

Using AIM will do two things for Matt's meeting. First, it will provide deeper insights for his client. Second, it will give Matt a list of problem questions from different angles. From this list Matt can converge on the catalytic questions—those questions that, if answered well, will resolve the client's itch.

The Power of Catalytic Questions

Catalytic questions zero in on, reframe, refine, or redefine a client's situation. At first the idea of a salesperson coming up with a catalytic question might seem counterintuitive. Doesn't the company already *know* these things? After all, it's their business. But our experience suggests that people often haven't looked deeply enough. They *assume* they understand their core issues, but often they don't.

We call this the Great Answer–Wrong Question syndrome. And it's remarkably common. You've probably experienced it yourself, either personally or in your company. You *think* they've identified the right issue. You work hard to answer it, and then you discover that . . . nothing's changed! The truth is that unless you ask the right question, it doesn't matter how good the rest of your work is. As Charles Kettering, the famed inventor and head of research for GM, put it, "A problem well stated is a problem half solved."

Catalytic questions provoke interest, clear away the fog, open the door to novel solutions, and motivate desire to act. That's why they're so powerful.

Catalytic questions are open ended. Like the open-ended questions above, they take a specific form—"How might you . . . ?" and "How *else* might we . . . ?" Notice that catalytic questions don't ask about the way things are done, but about the ways they *might* be done. They are future-oriented. Notice also that the second question above, "How *else* might we?," suggests the possibility of many answers. The *else* is designed to help you and your client dig deeper.

Because they are future-oriented, catalytic questions are, by definition, those your client *doesn't* already have answers for. They require imagination to answer, and, if answered well, they have the potential to resolve your client's itch.

Let's go back to the information Matt gathered while working with Ray. Here are some of the issues Matt listed in his Q-Notes:

- How might we minimize the time and effort required to approve shipments?
- How might we approve shipments in twenty-four hours?
- How might we automate approvals?
- How might we preauthorize shipments?
- How might we demonstrate more respect to inconvenienced staff?
- How might we cut out inefficiencies?

When you think you're close to a catalytic question, simply offer it to your client. This is very different from offering an idea, which can start the *suggest* → *object* → *defend* cycle. If your question reframes the situation in a new or useful way, your client will almost always react. People generally respond strongly when they hear issues framed in new and possibly useful ways.

If your client *doesn't* pick up on your question, don't defend. Instead, ask how he might phrase it. "I like to express challenges as questions to be answered. It implies that there is an answer out there somewhere, and it's just a matter of finding it. I'm thinking of one of your questions as something like, *How might we speed up shipping approvals?* but you might have a more accurate way of expressing it." Asking the client to explain the situation by defining the catalytic question can help you understand how they see the problem, and give you a new perspective on their challenge.

Simply identifying and communicating the catalytic question(s) is valuable to your client. Once you've done so, you have three options:

- *Go deeper.* If you don't yet have novel ideas to resolve the catalytic question, or if you are still unclear about the situation, explore it further to see if there is any way you can help.
- *Go wider.* If you do understand the situation, and have novel ideas for addressing it, note them in your Q-Notes so you can return to them at the end of the meeting. Then move to another area to explore— other itches that may stimulate new catalytic questions.
- *Move on.* If you've covered the critical areas, identified relevant catalytic questions, and have novel ideas to resolve them, you're probably ready to move into Act III of your meeting.

In our example, Matt elected to go deeper. He was curious about saving time on shipment approvals and wanted to know how Ray might be thinking. "Would it be fair to say that a summary of that issue is, *How might we minimize the time and effort required to approve shipments?*"

"Yes, that says it well."

Matt had already thought about subcontracting the approvals process, but he recognized it wasn't the core issue. He wanted to find something more compelling.

By probing Impediments with AIM, Matt generated several other problem questions, like *How might we use unregulated products?* And, *How might we reduce our need for high-density compounds?* These questions defined the challenge from a more technical perspective, perhaps introducing an angle Ray hadn't yet considered.

Ray was intrigued. "There is a market for products made with lower-density compounds, though we've avoided it because margins are lower. But new technology is out there that makes lower-density compounds more cost-efficient so the potential is there."

Ray was energized by exploring territory he hadn't previously considered. By simply identifying catalytic questions for his client, Matt provided value.*

The Power of Analogizing

Matt was ready to move on to other areas. "I have some thoughts on how you might be able to leverage lower-density compounds that I'd like to share with you in a few minutes. But first, can we go back to what you said about unhappy employees?"

"Sure."

"You said before that unhappy employees will always demand their pound of flesh. I was thinking we all have a little bit of *The Merchant of Venice* in us. It's a kid's game, really, isn't it? When we're unhappy, we take it out on our parents."

Ray laughed. "Tell me about it. I have three kids, eight, eleven, and fourteen."

"Me too. My youngest just went off to college."

You might be wondering why Matt decided to take a left turn here. Hasn't he already finished the small-talk part of the meeting? But there was method in Matt's shifting gears. He saw an opportunity to use another powerful Productive Selling tool—analogizing.

For many people, the term "analogy" might bring painful memories of high school English class: "All the world's a stage"; "A house divided against

---

*In *The Innovator's Dilemma,* Clayton Christiansen explains that as steam shovel companies began to focus exclusively on building large, expensive machines, they ceded the market for smaller machines to companies using hydraulics. Over time, hydraulics became more sophisticated, eventually replacing steam on even the largest shovels. Matt's catalytic questions might have opened similar insights for Ray. If lower-density compounds become more efficient, they might replace higher-density products, possibly creating new markets.

itself cannot stand." But metaphors and analogies aren't just the realm of Shakespeare and Lincoln. They're the way people think.

Cognitive scientists George Lakoff and Mark Johnson argue that metaphors and analogies help us express reality. They are fundamental mechanisms of the mind that allow us to use what we know about our physical and social experience to provide understanding of countless other subjects. And they're so powerful that they can shape our perceptions and actions without our even noticing them.*

Analogies are efficient. In just a few words, they can help us understand things that might otherwise take paragraphs to explain. *She's a rock; he has a moral compass; there are plenty of fish in the sea*—all of these convey their meanings vividly and quickly. Metaphor and analogy aren't unusual. They are as common as your morning coffee (oops—there's another one).

Let's see where Matt is going with his analogy. "So what do you do when you've let your kids down?"

"Well, with the two younger ones, we create a 'special surprise' and build up expectations around it."

"Maybe you could do something similar for your Maryland line workers."

Matt jumped to offering an idea. Generally, he offers ideas only at the end of a meeting. So this was either an exception, since the analogy was warm (if he suggested this idea later, he'd have to reset the context), or he was ready to move into Act III. Ray immediately picked up on Matt's idea. "A softball game. The line versus the suits. Not bad. With a cookout and a keg. They'll beat the pants off us, most likely. But we'll all win in the end."

Matt might offer to sponsor the keg, or simply be pleased he's given Ray his idea. His analogy (comparing the company to a family) created new insight into a situation—how the company might offer "special surprises" to show they regret the inconvenience and value the line's commitment.

---

*George Lakoff and Mark Johnson, *Metaphors We Live By* (Chicago: University of Chicago Press, 1980).

I n Act II of your sales conversation, you deliver value to your client in two ways *without prematurely offering your ideas.* You do this by practicing two techniques virtually guaranteed to keep your conversation lively, balanced, and nourishing. The first is identifying catalytic questions—to help your clients articulate the most useful problems to solve. The second is analogizing—to help your clients see their issues with new eyes.

Since the most accessible analogies are those based on personal experience, analogizing is also a way of sharing personal information about yourself and learning personal information about your client. Matt's analogy about kids and authority prompted Ray to mention his kids' ages. Matt also implied that he's recently become an empty nester (*My youngest just went off to college*). That might spark questions from any parent about transitioning to life without dependents.

The personal information Matt offered through his analogy is a platform for a possible relationship—and opportunities to follow up with his client. Next time Matt talks with Ray, he'll definitely ask about the kids. Matt likes kids and likes being a dad. He's interested. That's why he made the analogy he did. Asking about kids is entirely in Matt's character. It's who he is.

Analogizing has another value. Although questions are the heart of Act II, you don't want your meeting to feel like an interrogation—with you firing question after question at your client. Offering personal information and insights through your analogies is an organic way of contributing to the conversation. (Your scripts come in handy here too. If there's a natural opening for a piece of information about you or your company, drop it in. As long as it's relevant and short, it will offer information and vary the dynamic of the meeting from question-answer, question-answer to more of a natural conversation.)

Analogizing is powerful, but be careful not to overdo it. If you spend your entire meeting spouting things like, "That's like the shipping industry," or, "That reminds me of French Impressionism," or, "That's like training a puppy," you'll turn your client off faster than green grass through a goose.

Recap of Matt's Meeting Dialogue

Matt's research turned up some topics for the meeting. He entered the meeting with these topics populating the upper-left-hand corner of his Q-Notes page—Questions to ask. That was the content he wanted to explore. Matt then employed disciplined curiosity, supplemented by a series of tools to make sure he was thorough. He used the tools High Five, Open-Ended Questions, and AIM. He started with High Five, the most basic of the tools to explore the initial itch, the impact of the situation, identify other key stakeholders involved, find out why it's important, and uncover the values it links to for the client personally and organizationally.

To explore his client's situation more deeply, Matt then used Open-Ended Questions. He had some ideas, but instead of offering them as statements, he turned them into open-ended questions that stimulated further thinking and discussion.

Finally, to focus on those areas that might produce catalytic questions— questions that could reframe the way his client thinks about his issues— Matt used the AIM tool.*

As his client started to generate some ideas, Matt noted his own thinking in the upper-right-hand corner of his Q-Notes. He'll offer the best of those ideas at the end of the meeting.

Matt identified a number of possible catalytic questions, though he likely said only a few of them out loud. He analogized, making the reference to teenagers. The analogy created a couple of ideas that Matt will also bring up in the third third of his meeting. He also used the analogy to trade

---

*Once you become proficient at using these questioning tools, you'll find it may not be necessary to use them in the order we've presented them here. For example, once you've identified an itch with High Five, you may want to probe it further with AIM, and then decide to explore who is most affected by the itch by returning to the "Who's involved?" questions in High Five. Once you've unearthed the basic facts (with closed questions that can tell you things like how long your client has had the itch, how much it's costing, and so on), you'll probably want to focus on Open-Ended Questions. The more competent you become at using the tools, the smoother they will flow for you. As with any new skill, it takes time to develop competence. We recommend starting your development by going through the tools in order, until you become comfortable enough to use them more naturally. It's a little like learning to ride a bike. At first, you do everything by the book, trying to become consciously competent of each step. Eventually, you ride the bike without even thinking about the steps. You've become unconsciously competent.

personal information about being parents. He noted anything he learned about his client from these disclosures in the lower-left-hand corner of his Q-Notes—Key information. He'll use this information to create future personal touch points. Matt will use them as icebreakers in future correspondence, phone calls, and meetings.

What Matt did *not* do was talk about his product, make suggestions, or offer ideas. He stayed in the question.

Why Use Process Tools

Have you ever had the experience of beginning to explore an area with your client and not having a next question? One natural fallback when there is dead air is just to start commenting on the situation. But a better fallback is to ask a question drawn from the process you are following. If you are employing High Five and the conversation hits a lull, just follow the High Five process. "So how does this situation impact your business?" Sometimes it feels funny to ask a process-driven question. But we've never had a client balk at one. It usually feels better when your curiosity fuels your questions. But if your curiosity fails you in the moment, use your process. That's why you have one.

n the next chapter we'll see how you can demonstrate your value to your client by delivering USE-fulness. But first, let's take a break . . .

CHAPTER 17

Interlude—Give Yourself a Break

If at first you don't succeed—take a break.

—Jane

Where do you get your best ideas?

We often ask this question of participants in our innovation and sales training programs. Typical answers are *while exercising, in the car, while walking, in bed*. And more than 60 percent of our participants tell us that one of the top three places they get their best ideas is *in the shower.*

We often get our best ideas when we're not focused on getting ideas at all. Our minds perform remarkably well without supervision. This is a well-known cognitive phenomenon called incubation: you steep yourself in your challenge, take a break from actively thinking about it, and—boom—you come up with the answer. Leonardo, Gandhi, Marie Curie, and Einstein all used incubation to generate their most brilliant breakthroughs. And so can you.

"Sure," you might be thinking. "I've often gone to bed with a problem and woken up the next morning with the solution. But I can't very well doze off in the middle of a sales meeting."

Actually you can—in a way.

All you need to do is start moving. In fact, one of the most powerful ways to incubate is to take a walk. And there are two ways to do that in your meeting.

Ask for a Tour

Ask your client to take you for a walk. Just say, "One thing I'd like to do while I'm here is get a quick tour of your office [or facility]."*

When you go on a tour lots of good things can happen:

First, almost instantly, your relationship with your client changes. A moment ago you were a salesperson; now you're a guest. Your client is your host, telling you things with pride (or concern) that didn't come up in your sit-down meeting. People in the office will often notice you and remember you. Even months after a tour, we've often heard people say things like, "I remember. Elena was showing you around the office right before Christmas."

Second, there's a good chance you'll meet people—the CEO, CFO, even an old college pal (it's happened to us more than once). Your client may introduce you to people who are relevant to your business.

Third, by walking through your client's premises, you'll understand more about their business. You'll get a physical sense of what goes on. You'll see how people work and what processes they use, such as charts and drawings. You might even see what they produce. And there's a good chance you'll discover areas of the organization you hadn't been aware of. You will almost certainly get new ideas from the things you see.

Fourth, your tour can be a perfect opportunity to incubate. While you're walking, the pressure to "keep the meeting going" is reduced. In a sit-down meeting, a silent spell of more than a few seconds can be awkward, but a little silence as you walk down the hall together is perfectly acceptable. That silence lets your brain work in the background—incubation at its best.

And finally, being on the move also offers a natural way for you to shift back to small talk. Both you and your client might have exchanged information during your premeeting that piqued your curiosity. She might have mentioned a family vacation to South America that you didn't ask about. Now you can.

---

*If your meeting is in a conference room, and if it feels right to you, you might want to ask to see your client's workspace as part of the tour.

Use the Facilities

If a tour is inappropriate or inconvenient, you can always ask to use the washroom. The john is a time-tested incubation environment (remember our "Where to Get Your Best Ideas" survey).

Your trip to the bathroom gives you a chance to let your mind make those natural connections that can produce a useful insight.

And remember that while you're in the washroom, your *client* also has a chance to be alone for a few minutes—a chance to incubate. If you've been meeting with a group, they'll probably even talk about you, which might produce positive results. "Should we give Jane a rundown on the St. Louis deal, and see if she has any ideas?"

Timing

Ideally, you'll want to time your break just before you transition to Act III of the meeting, when both you and your client have collected enough grist for your incubation mill. Once the break is over, you have an excellent opportunity to recap where you are, raise additional points that might have occurred to you, and move to the final part of the meeting.

Obviously, an Interlude isn't right for every meeting. You need to use your judgment. If you have less than thirty minutes with your client, using five of them for a bathroom break may not be the best idea.

Whatever kind of Interlude you take—the tour, the walk to lunch, a coffee break—keep in mind that the simple act of moving is a chance for both you and your client to incubate or return to small talk. Think of your Interlude as "sales by walking around."

Mental Breaks

We think the best breaks involve moving around. But even if you can't take a physical break, you can still take a mental one—with a good analogy. Creating an Interlude with an analogy has several pluses.

A personal analogy can change the temperature of a meeting. When Matt used his analogy to bring families and children into the conversation with Ray, he created a productive break in the tone and intensity of the conversation.

An analogy can also bridge between status shifts. In Act II, you are largely in question-asking mode—a lower status than your client, who is the expert, answering the questions. In Act III, you'll want to step into the role of an adviser, offering ideas and suggestions—a higher status role. Because offering analogies that share personal perspectives is a peer status activity, it can be a useful way to ease into a higher status role.

CHAPTER 18

The Conversation, Act III—Be Useful

"Always be closing" is a great motto if you want to end a relationship.
If you want to grow one, try "Always be useful."

—Matt

The strategic objective of your sales conversation is to demonstrate value to your clients, to show them how you can help solve their problems or move them forward in some way. And just as in a movie or play, timing is critical. *When* you choose to deliver value is nearly as important as what you deliver. So wait. Wait until the final third of your meeting. Wait until Act III.

The Power of Waiting

At some level, we have all experienced the power of waiting. We know that love is more exhilarating when delayed, food more satisfying when we are hungry, accomplishment more rewarding when the task takes time. Even in sports, a victory in the final minutes of a game is far more galvanizing than a blowout that's obvious from the start. So too in sales: delivering value is more powerful at the end of your meeting than at the beginning.

In chapter 1, we introduced the concept of the third third. Researchers found that the ideas generated at the end of a brainstorming session are more creative—and ultimately more productive—than those generated early on. That's largely because the early ideas aren't so much the product of original insight as they are of memory. We spout out the things we remember, the things that are familiar, the ideas everyone has already had before. It's usually at the end of the meeting, based on the content of the discussion, that we begin to make new and potentially useful connections between problems and innovative solutions.

There is a similar dynamic in a sales meeting. If you've done your work well, by the time you make the transition to Act III, you are truly *ready* to deliver value. At the end of the meeting, you have a wealth of data to connect your knowledge, your products, and your network to your client's situation and issues. It's then that you can be the most useful.

Be of USE

The theme of Act III of the sales conversation is *to be of use.* You demonstrate usefulness by connecting your client with an array of insights—the key ideas you generated during your earlier exploration. All the threads of the meeting you orchestrated come together and you create a long list of value links.

We use the acronym U-S-E to capture the three types of value you can deliver.

- **Understanding**—the novel perspectives and insights you generated about your client's issues. You deliver Understanding by restating the catalytic questions and analogies you discovered during the meeting.
- **Sourcing**—the third-party goods or services that can help your client move forward on the needs you've identified, whether business or personal. You deliver Sourcing by offering to connect your client with people in your network.
- **Exchanging**—your own products, services, and ideas for resolving your client's needs. You deliver Exchanging by initiating a transaction. Note that Exchanging is a subset of Sourcing: Sourcing connects your clients with people or companies that can help them; Exchanging connects clients with your own products or services. Clearly, Sourcing doesn't earn you direct income while Exchanging does.

Nevertheless, the long-term value of Sourcing cannot be overestimated. It's one of your most important relationship builders.

Let's go into more detail about the three ways of delivering value to your clients.

Understanding

Providing Understanding is using your knowledge, wisdom, and intellect to deliver value. In a sense it's like coaching—you offer your client ways to see things differently—and usefully. You might even help them redefine their challenges. When you deliver value through Understanding, you may note a status shift in your conversation. As a provider of insight and wisdom, you are moving into a more elevated role.

Jane was exploring a relationship with a big-box consulting firm. Near the end of her first meeting, her client had to step out of the office to join a short conference call. Jane took that moment to make a list of all the challenges, from the client's perspective, she had uncovered in their conversation. It was a Productive Thinking summary of the meeting—a list of "How might we . . . ?" questions. As she finished the list, her client's assistant came in and apologized that her boss had a crisis to deal with and couldn't rejoin her. Jane left the list of her twenty most powerful "How to . . . ?" questions on her client's desk. He called her the next day. "That list you left me last night? That's exactly what we should be doing for our clients."

The only thing Jane did to deliver value was to generate a list of possible catalytic questions, and her client was intrigued. Not a bad impression to leave. A catalytic question brings value to your client before it's even answered. That's because it zeroes in on, reframes, or defines your client's situation. All by itself, the catalytic question provides insight and provokes curiosity. And the best part is, catalytic questions are not as difficult to find as you might think. Once you get used to asking "How might we . . . ?" questions, you'll discover a vast resource of potential catalytic questions—those questions that can give your clients an opportunity to see their issues in new and often useful ways.

Because of circumstance, all Jane could do was leave her list of catalytic questions. But in so doing, despite not even being there, Jane delivered the value of Understanding to her client. You can bet she walked into her next meeting with a healthy head start on her sale.

Like catalytic questions, good analogies can help clients see their situations from new perspectives. If helpful analogies surfaced during your meeting, touch on them again in Act III.

Delivering Understanding Before Act III

Many sales cycles revolve around a single pivotal meeting. In those cases, you will certainly want to wait to deliver your insights until Act III. However, in more complex situations, you'll probably meet several times in the course of a sales cycle. In those cases, your transition to Act III may not even occur during the first meeting. You may have to digest the details of your client's business or specific situation. Your client may not have answers to your questions readily at hand. There may be the need to involve other people on your client's side—or yours. You may need to explore further. Your client may want to take a deliberate approach to the process. Each of these variables, and more, will have an impact on how far you'll go in a first meeting.

Still, you want to leave your client with something that foreshadows the value to come. So if the sales cycle is long, the client's situation is complex, and your meeting ends before you can get into Act III, try to anticipate your next meeting by simply stating or restating the catalytic questions you've developed. Like Jane, you'll probably find a receptive audience—and a willingness to meet again.

Whether at the start of Act III or, in the long-cycle sale, in anticipation of it, articulating catalytic questions for your client demonstrates that you listened and synthesized their situation. It refocuses your client on the key questions that define a situation with greater clarity, or from a different perspective. And it articulates the problems you can help solve and creates anticipation for the cascade of ideas you will be bringing to the table.

Sourcing

Sourcing means connecting and introducing your client to resources, people, and information that can help them resolve their most pressing needs.

By delivering these connections you demonstrate that you are prepared to expend time and energy to help your client in ways that don't make you money directly. If your clients hire a freelancer you recommended or partner with an equity source you've connected them with, you've provided them with real, tangible value. It's unlikely they will forget you.

There are many ways to offer Sourcing to your clients—providing market information, a relevant news article or URL, running an analysis for them, introducing them to a potential partner, supplier, or client. Anything you noted in Quad 2 of your Q-Notes (where you listed ideas for helping your client that you uncovered during both your research and your conversation) or Quad 4 (where you recorded opportunities for further contact with your client) can be an opportunity to offer Sourcing.

During her meeting with a new client, Jane learned that the Quebec market was presenting unique challenges. The French spoken in Quebec and the French spoken in France are quite distinct. French Canadians are sensitive to this difference, and naturally prefer their own brand of French. Here's how Jane offered Sourcing, based on one of her catalytic questions.

"Earlier we were talking about your foray into Quebec and how you might overcome your lack of capacity for speedy translation into Quebecois. A Montreal friend of mine, who worked in our industry for ten years, now runs a small translation agency. He knows both Quebecois *and* our industry lingo. Would it be helpful if I put you in touch with him?" Jane knew her suggestion would fit a need. She thought of her translator friend when the subject first came up. But instead of suggesting it then, she wrote it in Quad 2 of her Q-Notes, and then waited to deliver her idea (a perfect example of the power of waiting). She won't earn any money from this recommendation, but she'll earn something ultimately far more important—her client's good-will and the recognition that she's delivered value.

Exchanging

Exchanging means aligning or matching one or more of your client's needs to your product, service, or execution. It's an exchange of value that includes you and your offerings. It's how you earn money through your relationship.

There are three primary types of values you can offer by Exchanging:

- Helping to mitigate some annoyance or discomfort the client is experiencing (resolving an itch your client articulated)
- Offering an economic advantage in the form of reduced costs or increased revenue (identifying and resolving an itch your client may *not* have articulated)
- Addressing industry drivers or company initiatives with a product or service you can provide (delivering *strategic value* against an itch your client may or may not have articulated)

In the last chapter Matt uncovered Ray's problem with red tape. Here's how Matt offered a catalytic question to propose his ideas.

"Earlier we identified an issue that I'll summarize as, How might you minimize the time and effort required to approve shipments? One of my other clients, a good friend I've been supplying for eight years, had a similar issue. It was driving him crazy. So we worked together to build a fast-track shipment release program. The key was preapproving six shipments over the next twelve months. We worked with the FDA to iron out the kinks. It still takes a fair bit of administrative time at the front end, but now they need to submit only a one-page form before shipments can be en route. It still requires three signatures, but they can be scanned. As long as they match the signatures in the security system, no problem—and no chasing executives all over the country for live signatures. I can pull together the details to go over them with you next week if you like. When might be good?"

If Matt can deliver on what he's promised, he's probably got a deal. Matt will bring whomever he needs to the detail meeting next week.

USE or UES?

USE is a mnemonic, not a hard-and-fast sequence. You can mix up the order in which you deliver value.

Jane feels most natural offering ideas for Exchanging as soon as she can. "I'm there to sell. They know that. After I confirm Understanding, I always follow up with one of my best Exchanging ideas." Matt, on the other hand, is more comfortable offering a Sourcing idea before moving into Exchanging. "I'm thinking about the relationship first, not the immediate opportunity. In the long run a strong relationship generates business." Neither approach is right. Neither is wrong. As always, the people, the issues, and the context will dictate what works best.

Whichever order works best for you and your situation, Sourcing first, then Exchanging, or the other way around, we recommend that you *start* with Understanding. By doing so, you'll not only be offering val ue to your client (relevant insights are significant value deliverers), you'll be giving yourself a chance to gauge whether you're on the right track.

At the end of your meeting, after you've offered your most powerful ideas for Exchanging, you may also find it useful to offer a final insight (U) or connection (S). Offering value that doesn't earn you money is a memorable way to end your meeting.

Don't Defend at the End

If your client shows no interest in your idea, or even objects to it, don't make the mistake of trying to defend it (remember the death spiral of *suggest* → *object* → *defend*?). Instead, simply move down your list. If you're not hung up by your own ego, it's easy to do. First, let go of your attachment to an idea that's going nowhere. Then reset the context by restating a catalytic question or recalling an analogy. And then simply propose your next idea. Remember, one of the reasons you waited till the end to present your ideas was to be prepared for this very possibility. By this point in the meeting, you should have a long list of options to offer.

Here's an example of how Jane avoided the dreaded *suggest* → *object* → *defend* spiral while mentoring a protégé, Nikki, a young marketing professional, who was moving to Houston and looking for a job.

Nikki had mentioned that she had a friend who knew people in the Houston marketing world. Jane offered some advice. "Ask for informational interviews with one or more of your friend's friends, then at the end of the meeting ask if there's anyone else who might be a good contact for you. Follow up with the new contact and keep your referrer informed. Do the same with each new referral, and in no time you'll have a web of people you can check in with. You'll be making natural contacts and staying in their headspace."

Nikki replied, "I'm not comfortable with that. I don't want to get a job through contacts. I'd rather know I got it because I'm the best candidate."

Jane could have said, "Look, if you're three people removed from your original contact, and you get a job, it's because of you, not the referral."

Instead, she said, "So I hear you saying you don't want to be the beneficiary of favoritism. Under what circumstances, where you began with a contact, would you feel comfortable that you earned the job on your own merit?"

Jane didn't defend her original suggestion. Instead, by asking an open question, Jane helped Nikki clarify her thoughts, and possibly see that her constraints might be self-imposed. Jane was being useful—delivering value, whether or not Nikki eventually acted on her advice.

Understanding your client's point of view is much more useful than convincing them how "right" you are. Instead of defending your idea with a declarative statement, or asking a yes-or-no question, ask an open "How might you . . . ?" question, and move on.

Confirm Your Assumptions

Jane had done a good job of exploring her client's needs in Act II, and time was getting short, so she checked Quad 2 of her Q-Notes, which was now filled with the USE connections she'd made. She was ready to open the floodgates.

"We only have about ten more minutes. First, I want to thank you for indulging my questions and for your thoughtful responses. I want to talk about some of the connections I've made based on what you've told me today. Is that okay?"

"Fire away."

"You mentioned you've been having a hard time filling your staff needs in Cape Town and that your team there is stretched to the breaking point. Did I get that right?" Jane was checking her facts and reminding her client of the problem she wanted to address.

"Actually, that problem will be solved soon. We have four new hires ready to start next month."

Discovering that a client problem isn't as critical as it first sounded isn't unusual. Jane had had a Sourcing idea, but now, because she restated the problem, she learned it was no longer relevant. Her strategy is simple, open, and effective: acknowledge the new information, then move to the next idea on her list. "I'm sure that's a relief. You also mentioned your concern that each of your satellites was developing its own culture around telecommuting. In my notes I wrote . . ." Jane will continue to move through her list, mixing Sourcing with Exchanging until she finds some useful matches. Her goal isn't to be right or to defend, but to be *useful*.

Whether Sourcing or Exchanging, offer your thoughts in a spirit of openness. If your client is interested, great. If they're not, you always have something else to offer.

Remember too that Sourcing and Exchanging are essentially the same thing—offering value. The only difference is that Exchanging makes you money, Sourcing doesn't—at least not directly. People tend to tighten up when money is at stake. That's natural, for both the client and the salesperson, but it can be especially uncomfortable for an inexperienced salesperson. Money often makes us start thinking of the meeting as a win-lose game. But if you walk into the meeting with the attitude that your goal is to be useful and to plant the seeds for a possible relationship, you can *always* find a win.

An unsuccessful meeting is one in which the salesperson fails to find any opportunities to deliver value. But because the concept of USE expands the value arena, you never have to have a failed meeting. Even in a brief meeting, or one that just begins to scratch the surface, or one where you see no immediate opportunity for Exchanging, you can almost always deliver value in at least one of the USE categories, and *delivering value is how you get remembered.*

Signs of Success

As you move through your list of ideas, you may find that if an idea is interesting, your client will begin to ask you questions. When your clients start questioning *you* about how, when, and where your product or service can help them, it's a wonderful sign that they see a connection between their problem and your solution.

Another strong hint that your meeting is successful (useful to your client) is when you say, "Looks like we have about ten more minutes," and your client replies, "It's okay. I can take some more time." Nobody will give you more time than they said they would unless you are providing value. When your client offers to extend the meeting, you know you're being of use.

Make Promises

The outcome of all the Sourcing and Engaging you do in your meeting is a series of promises. The word *promise* comes from the Latin meaning "to send forward." And that's exactly what a promise does. It propels a relationship into the future.

Promises don't always happen in a single meeting. Depending on your product, the complexity of your offering, and the industry in which you work, promising may be spread over (and between) a series of meetings. Whenever you offer them, however, the promises you make are what you've been working toward from the moment you first identified your client, through your premeeting research, through the small-talk Prologue to your meeting, and through all three acts of your sales conversation. The client needs you've discovered are the springboard for the Sourcing and Engaging promises you will make. And it's those promises that become the platform for the relationship you want to develop. Relationships are built on a foundation of promises that are made and kept.

Think of Sourcing and Engaging as opportunities to make promises:

- "I'll send you the link to that site we talked about."
- "As soon as I get back to the office, I'll send an e-mail introducing you and Harry."
- "Here are the six things I'll do in the next three weeks."
- "Let's meet at nine for coffee at the Bell in Hand Café."
- "I'll customize those agreements and get them to you in the morning."
- "I'll sign us up tomorrow for that 10k through the financial district on Saturday morning. Work for you?"

Your promises can be anything from "I'll walk the contract over this afternoon" to "I promise never to call you again," but whatever they are, be sure to *keep* them. Our philosophy on promises is simple: You don't *give* your word. You *are* your word. Once your clients know that, they know they can rely on you.

The last thing you do before standing up from a meeting is to get confirmation that you and your client are on the same page—that you each understand the promises you've made (and any promises your client may have made to you).

Being of USE to your client . . .

- *Proves you are a good listener.* When you organize and restate the six discussion points that were scattered over the last forty-five minutes, you demonstrate that you've truly heard your client. It's amazing how persuasive you can be just by listening.
- *Offers strategic understanding.* Catalytic questions are strategic questions. A pivotal step in good strategic thinking is identifying the critical gaps between where you are today and your goals. Asking catalytic questions demonstrates your capacity for strategic thinking.
- *Shows you can think laterally.* Analogies draw in related thinking from an unrelated universe. Edward De Bono calls this lateral thinking. It's one of the key thinking habits of creative problem solvers.
- *Assures you'll occupy a piece of your client's headspace.* The more Sourcing connections you can make that address your client's challenges, both business and personal, the more you'll pop into a client's thoughts.
- *Keeps you from overselling.* By having a list of ideas for your client from all three USE categories, you can avoid the natural tendency to defend the one idea you're "sure" is the perfect solution for your client's needs.

What About Closing Techniques?

As we said way back in chapter 1, you won't find information about closing techniques in *Never Be Closing.* We're keeping that promise. Closing techniques, especially those designed to manipulate clients into saying yes when they're not yet persuaded or ready, are diametrically opposed to the Productive Selling philosophy.

We don't think it's ethical to pressure clients into buying. Even if it were, we seriously doubt that closing techniques would be very effective— certainly not in the long run. Most people aren't stupid. Even if you succeed in using psychological gimmicks to pressure someone to buy when they don't want to, you may get the sale, but it's unlikely you'll get a second one. You'll be remembered as the person who fulfilled the worst stereotypes of salespeople.

In the end, we doubt these closing techniques work very often anyway. One common gambit is to ask a series of questions designed to induce a yes. After several yes responses, the seller asks a question like, "Shall we go over the contract?" Presumably, the series of yes answers will induce another yes, and, voilà, you've closed.* We find it hard to believe that with big-ticket items, gimmicks like this are effective. If the client buys, it's likely he was ready to buy. And if the client isn't ready to buy, it's likely he won't. In either case the salesperson comes off as disingenuous.

The best way to be a good closer is to be an incisive questioner, a creative problem solver, and a reliable promiser. If you figure out how your product or service is useful to your clients, they will ask to buy. The best way to close a deal is by asking: "Do you want to move to the next step?"; "Should I draft a contract?"; "What additional information do you need before we draw up an agreement?"; or similar questions. Such questions are overt, not manipulative. They are transparent, not techniques. Closing is as simple as that.

Our experiences suggest that once you engage your client in his vision and restate how you might help him achieve it, the sale virtually makes itself. At the very least, you'll have won the privilege of being welcomed the next time you call.

Conclude the Meeting

In the same way your meeting started before the first hello (remember chapter 14 about the meeting before the meeting?), it doesn't end with good-bye. There's one more critical task you need to perform before you can consider your meeting officially over.

Your meeting isn't over until you've rewritten your notes to make sure

---

*In closing-oriented sales books, this is sometimes referred to as the tie-down technique.

they are legible. You purposely used short forms when taking notes during the meeting so you could focus on your client. The longer you wait to transfer your scribblings, the more your notes page will look like gibberish to you in the days and months ahead. Turn your cryptic notes into legible sentences. This will not only help you understand what you wrote but also refresh your memory about what was discussed so you can communicate it more clearly to others. You can also take the opportunity to add any new thoughts that occur to you, in the appropriate quadrant.

We think this advice is so important, we'll repeat what we said at the end of chapter 11, where we introduced the concept of Q-Notes: *Always schedule time as soon as possible after your meeting (within an hour or two at most) to rewrite your meeting notes in detail. Always.* Consider the time it takes to do this as part of your meeting time. Consider it part of the investment you make in yourself and your sales process. Consider it an indispensable part of selling better. Rewrite your notes as completely as you can, as soon as you can.

PART V

After the Meeting

CHAPTER 19

Do Not Skip This Section—
Make the Most of Your Meeting

Without work one finishes nothing. The prize will not be
sent to you. You have to win it.

—Ralph Waldo Emerson

There's an old saying that every meeting is really three meetings: the one you plan for, the one you have, and the one you replay in your head. Replaying your meeting, congratulating yourself on the high points, and fretting over the low ones is natural. But unless you apply the rigor of a structured debrief, it won't be very useful.

The chapters in this section outline a deliberate debriefing methodology designed to help you get the most out of your meeting so that you can build on your successes, learn from your shortcomings, and do better next time . . . and the time after that . . . and the time after that.

- Chapter 20 offers a framework for debriefing the *process* of your meeting—how you orchestrated it to cross the credibility threshold, discover your client's needs, and demonstrate usefulness.
- Chapter 21 shows you how to extract the most from the *content* of your meeting—how to identify and leverage the information you gathered.
- Chapter 22 shows you how to use what you learned to build a relationship, stay in your client's headspace, and generate additional business.

We know from experience that even with the best of intentions, people (and entire organizations) are tempted to skip debriefing. The world moves fast. There's always another "next thing" on your plate. There's always a fire to put out. As a result, the first thing to go is often the time you've allocated to debrief.

And yet we also know that the greatest learning comes from taking the time to analyze what worked, what didn't work, and where to improve. In chapter 6, we discussed the success of the U.S. Army's OPFOR unit—a success largely attributed to the learning the group gets from its commitment to conducting highly structured After Action Reviews of all its activities.

Applying the lessons from those AARs is what makes OPFOR the most successful operating division in the military. Conducting your own structured process and content debriefs and then applying what you've learned will help you become the most successful salesperson you can be.

Read these chapters. Read them in order. Apply them to your work. We promise you'll benefit.

CHAPTER 20

After the Action—Debrief the Process

A professional is just an amateur who kept getting better.

—Jane

There are two kinds of debrief from which you will benefit. The first is the *process* debrief—taking a close look at how you conducted your sales conversation, what you did that worked well, what you did that could be improved, and other observations about the dynamics of the conversation. In other words, the *how* of the meeting. The second debrief you'll want to consider is the *content* debrief—analyzing what you learned from your client about their strategies, their challenges, and their needs. In other words, the *what* of the meeting.

Both debriefs are critical to your success. The *content* debrief will help you plan your next steps for building a relationship and winning business—so there's a good chance you'll see near-term benefits from this activity. The *process* debrief, on the other hand, will help you become a better salesperson. You'll likely see some results in the near term, small things you can tweak to make your presentation better, or cross the credibility threshold faster, or ask more effective catalytic questions. But the real benefits of the process debrief will be in the longer term, as you become more confident and comfortable with your developing skills—as you evolve into a truly productive salesperson.

Here's our advice: Do your process debrief first.

Since the content debrief holds the promise of immediate results, there will be a strong temptation to start there. But once you get drawn into pursuing the business possibilities you've uncovered, it will be difficult to go back and think about the things you did in the meeting that helped you reveal those opportunities. Because its true value lies further in the future, the process debrief becomes a classic example of a high-value, low-urgency task—otherwise known as "stuff we don't do."

We humans are funny. We almost always overestimate the value of what we can accomplish in the short term and underestimate the value of what we can accomplish in the long term. That all-too-human tendency results in lost opportunities for health, for wealth, for happiness, even for love. It's a risk you don't have to take when it comes to your career. You've already rewritten your Q-Notes, as we recommended at the end of chapter 17. You won't forget them. They won't disappear. Do yourself a favor and debrief your process first. It's work, for sure, and yes, you'll be itching to get to that content. But it's more than worth the effort. Regardless of your starting point, your process debriefs will help you become better at your craft.

Experiential Learning

The Experiential Learning Cycle is a theory of adult learning proposed by psychologist David Kolb.* According to Kolb, we learn most effectively when we reflect on our experience, use these reflections to develop new ways of thinking and behaving, and then test these approaches in new situations. This testing, in turn, creates new experiences, from which we can refine our models of thinking and acting. With each cycle of actively reflecting on our experiences, adjusting our models, and applying them to new situations, we enrich our skills and improve our outcomes.

The most basic way to use Kolb's theory is to ask three simple questions each time we reflect on an experience:

*David A. Kolb, *Experiential Learning: Experience as the Source of Learning and Development* (New Jersey: Prentice-Hall, 1984).

- What happened?
- What did it mean?
- What might be useful to do differently?

Or, in our short form:

- What?
- So What?
- Now What?

Debriefing with What? So What? Now What?

What? So What? Now What? is the overall structure we recommend for conducting a simple, but powerful, After Action Review.

To get the most out of this structure, we recommend learning and using three basic thinking tools—one for each stage of the debrief:

- Story Mapping to dig deeply into what happened (the *What?* of the debrief)
- POWER to understand its meaning (the *So What?* of the debrief)
- Start-Stop-Improve to determine what to do differently (the *Now What?* of the debrief)

What? (Story Mapping)

If you've followed our advice, one of the first things you did after your sales meeting was to review and rewrite your Q-Notes to be sure you understood all your shorthand scribbles and captured as many details of the meeting as possible.

You also know that sales meetings generally follow a three-act structure, often introduced with a Prologue and sometimes interrupted with an intermission of some sort. The Prologue usually consists of small talk. Act I is where you establish credibility. Act II is where you ask questions to discover the situation, the itches, and the challenges your client faces. And Act III is where you deliver value and demonstrate usefulness.

Act I and Act II contain turning points that drive you into the next act. In Act I the turning point is when you've established enough credibility to start asking questions. In Act II the turning point is when you've gathered enough information to articulate one or more catalytic questions or analogies that create the potential for delivering value to your client. Act III also contains a key point—the moment at the end of the meeting where you summarize the various promises you've made.

If you were to graph all these elements in an hour-long meeting, they might look something like this.

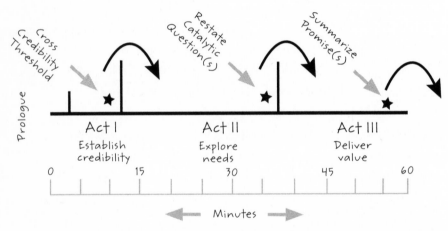

Your first step in Story Mapping is to draw a simple graph of your meeting, similar to the one above. Your timings will probably be different from the general ones above, so you should label each element of your graph with times that reflect the way your meeting actually flowed. Use your Q-Notes to refresh your memory. If you've jotted down times in your Q-Notes, constructing a reasonably accurate graph should be fairly easy.

Now, using your graph as a guide, answer the following questions to tell the story of your meeting:*

---

*Note that this is a starter list of questions. Over time, you will develop a list of questions that fit your own needs, your own style, your own industry.

- How did your meeting start off?
- What were the first things you and your client said to each other?
- What did you say in your Prologue small talk?
- What did you learn in your Prologue small talk?
- When did you move into Act I?
- What was the first thing you said in Act I?
- What was the first thing your client said in Act I?
- What clues did you notice to identify your client's thinking preferences (energizers)?
- How did you adjust your communication to connect with these preferences?
- What did you do to establish credibility in Act I?
- What else did you do to establish credibility in Act I?
- What status did you adopt in Act I?
- What was the turning point for moving into Act II?
- How did you know this was the turning point?

- What was the first thing you said in Act II?
- What was the first thing your client said in Act II?
- How did you begin to explore your client's situation, goals, itches?
- How and when did your client express interest or enthusiasm?
- How did you respond?
- How and when did your client express disinterest?
- How did you respond?
- What catalytic questions emerged?
- Who articulated each one, you or your client?
- What analogies emerged?
- Who articulated each one, you or your client?
- What status did you adopt in Act II?
- What was the turning point for moving into Act III?
- How did you know this was the turning point?
- Did you or your client create an Interlude?
- Were you able to return to small talk?
- What was the first thing you said in Act III?

- What was the first thing your client said in Act III?
- How did you refer back to your catalytic questions and analogies?
- How did you deliver Understanding?
- How did your client respond?
- How did you deliver Sourcing?
- How did your client respond?
- How did you deliver Exchanging?
- How did your client respond?
- How did you deliver promises?
- How did your client respond?
- How did your client deliver promises?
- How did you respond?
- How did you summarize the meeting?
- How did your client respond?
- What status did you adopt for the end of the meeting?
- What were the last things you said?
- What were the last things your client said?

As you tell the story of your meeting, using your chart and these questions as a guide, try not to make any value judgments. Try to recount the events of the meeting as objectively as you can.

Reviewing your meeting like this may feel awkward at first, and you may be tempted to shortcut some of the questions, thinking, "Oh, that's pretty obvious. . . . I know that. . . . I'll just skip down to the important stuff." *Don't!* There is irreplaceable value in digging into the details. It's this deliberate and uncompromising self-examination that is at the core of the AAR process used by OPFOR—and the reason OPFOR has such a remarkable track record.

If going through these questions feels awkward at first, find a colleague or friend to help you. Ask them to play the role of a reporter and simply ask you the questions. This will feel a lot more like a conversation and make it easier for you to recall what happened and what was said.

We strongly recommend that you make some kind of record of your meeting. You can take notes, write out your recollection in full, or voice-record it. Whatever method you choose, do record your memory of the meeting so you can refer to it later.

Finally, once you've told the story of your meeting, take a second look at your meeting graph and tell the story again, but this time from the point of view of your client. Don't go into the same level of detail, but try to see the meeting from your client's point of view. Look through your client's eyes. Hear with your client's ears. How might they characterize the meeting? As a good use of their time? As informative? As valuable? As enjoyable? As energizing? Why or why not? What might they have noticed about what you said, what you did, what they said and did? Again, try to avoid value judgments. Let your "client" tell the story as objectively as possible. Note the key differences, if any, between your version of the meeting and your client's version of the meeting.

Once you've completed your Story Mapping session—constructing a meeting graph and telling the story of your sales conversation from your perspective and from your client's perspective—you will have a pretty clear idea of what actually happened during the meeting. The next step is to extract salient lessons from the story. What did it all mean?

So What? (POWER)

POWER is a tool we could talk about for hours (but don't worry, we won't).* It's one of the most useful tools in the Productive Thinking and Productive Selling arsenal—though it's one your client will rarely see. POWER is ideal for distilling the meaning of what happened during your sales conversation— and for identifying what you have to do to become better at your craft. POWER is an acronym that stands for Positives, Objections, What Else, Enhancements, and Remedies. It's a structured way of analyzing and under- standing any activity—from an OPFOR battle maneuver to a sales meeting.

Page 208 shows a typical POWER sheet for analyzing a sales meeting.

A note about What Else: What Else is a catchall bucket. It's designed to make sure you don't miss anything. You can add What Else comments any- time during the POWER process. As you go through each of the other categories—Positives, Objections, Enhancements, and Remedies—it's likely that additional What Elses will occur to you. Throw them in the What Else bucket for now. Then review the list and sort its contents where they belong. You may decide that some items fit best in a different category.

When filling out a POWER sheet it's important not to censor yourself. Write down whatever occurs to you, whether it seems important or not. It's all too easy to think of an item and then say to yourself, "Oh, that's not really all that important." Defer your judgment. Write down anything and every- thing. That way you're less likely to miss a key item that might not have seemed important at the time, but that actually might have had a significant impact on the meeting.

In the end, you should have a robust list of Positives, Objections, Enhancements, and Remedies. And your What Else bucket will contain a few miscellaneous items that give you a new perspective on your experience.

*Our devotion to POWER reminds us of a story told by football coach John Madden (Bryan Burwell, *Madden: A Biography*, Triumph Books, 2011). In 1962, a twenty-two-year-old Madden attended a presenta- tion by Vince Lombardi. The subject was the Green Bay Packer Power Sweep. Madden expected Lombardi to talk about the Power Sweep for an hour or so and then move on to other topics. Madden was wrong. Lombardi talked for eight hours about that one play. He broke down every player's responsibility, offense and defense, for every possible defensive alignment. That's how we feel about our POWER tool. It's like the Green Bay Packer Power Sweep of structured creativity.

POSITIVES	**E**NHANCEMENTS
What was positive or useful about the way you managed the meeting? What did you do that moved the meeting toward success? What were your strengths? Where did you shine?	How might you enhance all the Positives you listed above? How might you make your performance even stronger, even more likely to succeed?
OBJECTIONS	**R**EMEDIES
What was problematic about the way you managed the meeting? What did you do that moved the meeting away from success? What were your weaknesses? Where did you stumble?	How might you overcome the Objections you listed? How might you eliminate or reduce your weaknesses and give yourself and your process a greater chance to succeed?

WHAT ELSE?

What Else occurs to you about the way you ran the meeting? About its ups and downs? Its pacing? The way you asked questions? The way you answered them? What else about how you bridged between thoughts? About how you catalyzed? How you analogized? What else about how you began the meeting? How you brought it to a close? About your small talk? What else about the unexpected occurrences during the meeting, both welcome and unwelcome, and how you handled them? What else about yourself, about your process, about your emotions?

Opposite is a POWER sheet for a recent meeting Matt held. (Yes, even a seasoned salesperson like Matt benefits from a structured process debrief. It's why he's so successful.)

Once you've completed your POWER exercise, your next step is to focus on the items you want to improve before your next meeting. And that's where you conduct the final part of your process debrief, Now What?

POSITIVES

Good things about how I ran the meeting
- Learned lots about J thru small talk, e.g., interest in strategy games.
- Bridged well to our waterfront devs, established my cred. J was intereseted.
- Small talk to cred in 2 mins flat. Love that!
- Chess analogy re complex waterfront bureaucracy clicked for him.
- Idea list at end engaged him. He sat right up.

ENHANCEMENTS

How to improve what was Positive
- Build on shared connection.
- Ask more Qs linking chess to J's work.
- Asked more about J's interest in game theory, how he uses it in his work.
- Be sharper about looking for differentiating Qs like that. Ideas guys respond strongly to challenging Qs.
- Take your time. No need to rush!

OBJECTIONS

Not so good things about how I ran the meeting
- Too slick? Transition from how I like Chicago to J's situation maybe too pat. How might I remain authentic, not appear plastic?
- Assuming cred by controlling meeting worked well, but maybe came on too strong. How might I demo cred strongly but still be more conversational?

REMEDIES

How to overcome each Objection
- Listen better! Chess wasn't the issue. Strategy was! Our work w Dr V on applying game theory to waterfront dev, would've been stronger. Listen for underlying interests, not surface interests.
- Develop industry driver comments as cred builder. Summarize 3–5 drives + my take + what others are doing to leverage trends, like higher cap requirements and energy costs.

WHAT ELSE?

Other observations about how I managed the meeting
- Jon is big ideas guy, maybe some energy for process in him too. Remember for future.
- Gaming analogy worked well. I can use that with other clients BUT (see Remedies).
- Sailing is a shared interest too. Could have vesd that to connect! Listen, listen, listen!

Now What? (Stop-Start-Improve)

Stop-Start-Improve is a way of converging on the actions you can take that will make the biggest near-term difference in the way you manage your sales meetings. The name of the tool says it all. Simply ask yourself the following: What should I *stop* doing? What should I *start* doing? What can I *improve* or do better?

If you've done a thorough job on the POWER tool, you may have a long list, or several long lists, of potential things you could change. But change is an ornery beast. If you try to change everything at once, you'll end up in chaos. So our first recommendation is to take a close, critical look at your POWER exercise and decide which changes you think have the greatest chance of success in the near term.

If you follow the Productive Selling approach, you'll conduct many Story Mapping and POWER exercises as you move through your career, and the incremental refinements you make with each one will add up to make a very large—even radical—improvement over time. Remember, we tend to overestimate what we can accomplish in the short term and underestimate what we can accomplish in the long term. Take small bites.

Let's see how Matt converts his POWER analysis into a workable set of actions through Stop-Start-Improve. His aim is to focus on those things he thinks might have the greatest impact.

Based on his POWER notes, Matt asks himself, "With respect to running sales conversations, what can I stop doing, what can I start doing, what can I improve (in other words, continue to do, but do better)? Here are the notes he writes himself. (Yes, we recommend you take notes again. This is important work. You don't want to forget it. And you'll want a record of your decisions that you can measure over time.)

Stop: Don't try to make a personal connection where there isn't one. Just because I know how to play chess (poorly) doesn't create common ground with a chess master. Be real. If there's a genuine connection, great. If not, don't manufacture one.

Matt is reminding himself to remain authentic. Of course he wants to make a connection, but it has to be genuine. Anytime you are inauthentic in a meeting, whether trying to make a connection, feign interest, or oversell your expertise, your client will smell it—probably before you do. It's not worth the risk to the relationship you want to build.

Start: Develop and practice a credibility-building industry insight script for skeptical prospects.

Matt knows that one of his strongest assets is his industry expertise and the insights he brings to the table. Anything he can do to build on those strengths will be useful. An industry insight script will also give him new questions to ask, such as: How do my clients think about these industry drivers? What can I learn from their insights? Do they have any strategic plans to leverage or mitigate changing drivers?

Improve: Listen better. Listening = focus. Try not to anticipate what comes next in the meeting. Stay in the present. Monitor doing this over time. Also, think about all my outside interests and build business analogies for them. Like sailing. Unprepared = risk. Small problem in calm lake, *big problem* in stormy sea. Analogies always useful.

Matt's good, but he's far from perfect. He knows he can get distracted—worrying about what might come next in the meeting rather than staying focused on what's actually happening. Listening better sounds simple, but it's not. It's the bedrock skill for any human interaction. As a people person, Matt knows that. He also knows he can do better. So he's decided to work on his listening skills. He knows it will make a difference—not only to his ability to sell but also to his ability to be useful over the long term.

Putting It All Together

The three steps in the process debrief aren't difficult. *What? So What? Now What?* are all straightforward questions.

The three tools to help you unpack those questions are also straightforward. Story Mapping helps you recall what actually happened, both from your point of view and from your client's. POWER helps you get a handle on the significance of what happened. And Stop-Start-Improve gives you a way to focus on the things you can do better next time.

While not complicated, the debrief takes time. You probably already invested at least several hours getting ready for your sales meeting. Doesn't it make sense to invest a little additional time to harvest the meeting's full value? Farmers spend a lot of time tilling their soil and planting their seeds. Most of that effort would go to waste if they didn't also invest time in harvesting.

Debriefing Other People's Stories

The sales world is full of stories, supposedly passing wisdom from one salesperson to the next. Sadly, much of the so-called wisdom is bogus. Without effective debriefing skills, it's easy to extract the *wrong lessons* from any given story. But the good news is that once you get good at debriefing and extracting the learning from your own stories, you can apply the same discipline to other people's stories—and draw truly useful lessons from them.

Here's a simple example.

Salesman Bob identified an opportunity he thought was perfect for a prospect of his. Bob was selling ad space for a TV documentary on sustainability. The theme of the show fit perfectly with his prospect's mission, and Bob could offer the ad space at a discount.

He called and left a message. It wasn't returned. Over the next forty-eight hours Bob called thirty-five more times, leaving fifteen unanswered voice mails. Finally, he got through to his prospect. She was so annoyed she told him never to call again.

Bob did phone again, the next day, and asked for one minute of her time. He laid out the premise and the price. She loved it and agreed on the spot to buy.

Bob filed this story under "perseverance." Over the years, he's told it hundreds of times. His tenacity resulted in a sale. But is that really the story's lesson? Let's debrief the story using a quick version of *What? So What? Now What?*

What? Bob called thirty-six times, leaving sixteen messages with his name and number. When he finally got through, his client told him never to call again. He called back anyhow and in one minute outlined the offer and price. The client was impressed and said yes.

So What? Using a mini version of POWER, we could run through Positives and Objections.

Positives: Being willing to call again after being told not to.
Outlining the offer and price in one minute.
Objections: Calling thirty-six times and leaving sixteen messages.

Now What? If sixteen callback messages resulted in no callbacks, and a one-minute script resulted in a sale, what might be a better strategy? After several unanswered messages, Bob could have left a short, intriguing, and *substantive* voice mail that gave his client a *reason* to call back. Something like: "The advertising opportunity is for a show about climate change. As I understand it, your mission is directly linked to the climate change issue." Bob might also have mentioned a price in his message.

Seen through the lens of the disciplined process debrief, the real take-away from the story is not the value of persistence but rather the importance of having a strategy for leaving quick, meaningful, and persuasive messages.

Whenever you hear an amazing sales story, don't simply take its supposed lesson at face value. A little disciplined process analysis might provide a gold mine of insight.

We strongly recommend the *What? So What? Now What?* discipline. It's a proven way to harness the power of the Experiential Learning Cycle, and it can help you become a more productive salesperson each time you use it.

CHAPTER 21

Mine the Meeting—Debrief the Content

Knowledge is about learning facts. Wisdom is about using them well.

—Matt

The purpose of your sales meeting was to give you the opportunity to learn who your client is as a person, what their goals are, the hurdles that stand in their way, and how you might be able to offer them ongoing value. Your sales conversation provided you with the raw data to achieve all these things, but to bring that data into focus so you can *act* on it, you need to conduct a deliberate content debrief. Unpack what you learned and filter it through your own capabilities and those of your organization so you can be clear on how to structure what you can offer, and what your next steps should be.

Your content debrief is the USE part of the meeting done again with the luxury of time, incubation, and additional minds. In your content debrief you want to:

- Get your team involved and enthusiastic
- Generate a long list of opportunities to recontact your client
- Build an action plan that delivers on the promises you made during the meeting and the followup ideas you developed

The following pages show how you and your colleagues can mine your Q-Notes, access your creativity, and design dozens of ways to demonstrate value, build relationships, and catalyze business. It's not rocket science. In fact, it's very simple. It's just that most salespeople don't do it. That's too bad, because following our three-step process can make the difference between a moderately positive sales experience and a truly great one—for both you and your client.

Step 1: Prepare for a Content Debrief Meeting

If you've followed our advice so far, you've already done part of this. You took the time to rewrite your notes as soon as possible after the meeting and to add any additional insights you might have had. You also retold the story of your meeting as part of your *process* review. As a result, you now have a pretty good handle on what happened. In fact, at the moment, you are the world's expert on that meeting. You know more about it than anyone else, including your client, simply because you've replayed it and analyzed it several times already.

Now take the time to review and edit your Q-Notes one final time with the intent of preparing a clean copy so that your team can follow along as you share your meeting with them and ask them to help you generate ideas to move forward.

Next, plan a debrief meeting. Treat it as you would any other important meeting.

- Dedicate an appropriate amount of time both for a presentation of what you learned *and* for discussion. We recommend forty-five minutes as a minimum, at least half of which should be allocated to discussion.
- Reserve a room with sufficient wall space for posting flip chart sheets and sticky notes.
- Invite the people who are invested (or who may *become* invested) in your success with this particular client. There are many

possible candidates—your analyst or a member of your support team, your product manager, the people responsible for servicing your client, others on your sales team who might benefit from what you learned, junior salespeople who may have fresh insights, marketing and communications people, or your boss. If you work in a small organization, you can be sure that almost all your key colleagues will be curious about your meeting, will appreciate a summary of what you learned, and may have useful insights to offer.

• Send your debrief team an invitation stating the time (including end time), place, and purpose of the meeting. Tell them that you will be reviewing what you learned and will be asking them for their ideas and insights about how best to move forward to capitalize on the opportunities you've uncovered.*

Step 2: Hold a Salestorm Meeting

We call the content debrief meeting a Salestorm—because that's exactly what it is. The purpose of your Salestorm is to tap into the experience and intelligence of your colleagues to generate ways of capitalizing on all the effort you've put in so far.

People who conduct regular Salestorms find that these sessions can become quite popular in their organizations. Your team will usually appreciate a summary of your sales meeting. It keeps them in the loop and expands their industry awareness. Innovation teams may be particularly interested because Salestorms are a way for them to get into the heads of potential users. And Salestorms are a great way to inject energy into your office environment, because good Salestorms are more than just information downloads—they're opportunities for people to offer their input.

---

*Be explicit that your meeting won't be just an information dump—that you need *their* ideas and opinions. You will get a better response if people know their input will be asked for and valued.

Here's how to conduct an effective Salestorm.

Make sure your meeting room has enough wall space or whiteboard area for people to post their thoughts, using Post-it notes. It's also helpful if the room has enough space for people to walk around freely. A cramped room often makes for cramped thinking. Give your team a supply of Post-it notes and fine-tipped markers so their writing will be large enough to read from a distance. Then introduce the meeting:

"Thank you all for making the time to be here. I'm hoping that as a result of our meeting, we'll be able to come up with useful ways to engage with a new client relationship I'm developing. I'm going to run through a recap of my meeting with Jim Worrall from Hadrian. Jim is responsible for Hadrian's Southwest operations. And I think we have some real potential with them. What I'm looking for is your help in figuring out how to create touch points with Jim and his team as we move forward. I'll try to be as brief as possible, but I want to give you enough detail to stimulate your ideas. As I go through what I've learned, I'd like you to use your Post-its to jot down anything you think I might have missed or anything at all that you think might be useful. Don't worry about whether your idea might be good or bad or relevant or irrelevant. Whatever you think of will be of value. Just write one idea or question or observation or insight per Post-it. Just capture anything that occurs to you—one idea per Post-it."

Then use your notes to run through a detailed recap of your sales conversation.

Once you've given the overview of the meeting, go through your Q-Notes, quadrant by quadrant. It can be useful to draw a rough four-quadrant Q-Note template on a whiteboard or flip sheet to give people a framework for posting their ideas. As you review the contents of each of your Q-Note quadrants, ask your team to offer their ideas as indicated below.

Ask your colleagues to write down anything that occurs to them that fits into any of the four quadrants, have them say it out loud, and then have them stick it up on the whiteboard or flip sheet. Capturing ideas on Post-its makes it easy to move them around, and create nodes or clusters that go together. The procedure is simple:

- Write it (legibly).
- Say it (so it can stimulate ideas from other people).
- Stick it up (so it's visible).

Questions to ask	Ideas to communicate
Ask your team if there are other areas or angles you should be curious about. What are the unanswered questions? List any new questions or areas that come to mind.	Ask your team if there are any additional USE ideas that might offer value to your client. List additional information that might be useful to offer the client.
Key information (personal/business) Ask your team to capture on sticky notes any additional information they think might be useful. Invite them to list questions they think you could have asked, or could still ask, your client.	**Reasons to follow up** Ask your team to generate additional ideas for following up with the client, whether business or personal. Remind them that one good personal touch point may do more to build a relationship than ten business ones.

There is no need for people to explain or defend what they write, or even to make sure it goes in the correct quadrant. What's important is to get the ideas up quickly so that they are visible and available for others to build on and discuss.

Once all the ideas are up, go through each quadrant with the team, focusing on new ideas for connecting with your client, and inviting people to discuss their thoughts, generate more ideas, and build on the ideas that have already been offered. In theory, every item in Quads 1 and 2 can be turned into a followup activity. Your aim is to create a long list of possible touch points between you and your client. Be sure to tell your team that you are not only looking for business touch points that immediately generate a return. Remind them that personal touch points and opportunities for Sourcing—even though these do not generate direct business—are just as important in terms of demonstrating usefulness and building a relationship.

Step 3: Design Your Plan

After you've gathered input from your Salestorm, your final step is to design a plan of action to follow up with your client. Your plan will consist of three items:

First and foremost, the promises (including delivery dates, if any) you made to your client during the sales meeting. Delivering on your promises, *when you said you would,* is critical to your credibility. If you told the client you'd send a market analysis and all they get from you is ballet tickets, they might be pleased, but they won't be impressed with your reliability.

Second, make a short list of the most valuable touch points, both business and personal, generated by you and your team.

Third, create a detailed schedule of touch point and followup activities, including who will do what by when. What tasks does your analyst have? What about your boss? Make sure to schedule your promises, as well as any time-sensitive ideas, as early as necessary. Create a calendar to track each touch point, with dates, responsibilities, and opportunities to note course corrections or other developments.

Commencement—Occupy Headspace

The reason success won't fall into your lap is
because you can't get it by sitting down.

—Virgil

I n the best-case scenario, the end of all your work—from writing your
scripts to researching your prospective client to getting your meeting to
conducting a second round of research to establishing credibility, exploring
your client's needs, and demonstrating usefulness, and all the way through
to your process and content debriefs—is not simply a sale but the beginning
of a relationship. That's why we call this chapter "Commencement."

You already know that we believe selling is a helping profession at its
core: the most successful salespeople are those who strive to understand
their clients' needs and who are always on the lookout for ways to provide
value. But it's not simply about being altruistic, being "a good guy," or enjoy-
ing spending time with people. At its core, our approach is highly pragmatic.
Anyone in business knows that it's almost always cheaper to get repeat business than to generate new business. It takes a lot less time, effort, and money
to convert an existing business into a new business than it does to make a
sale from scratch. From a business point of view, it makes a lot of sense to
find ways to occupy more territory in your client's headspace.

Headspace

Have you ever noticed that for some people, recognition and success
just seem to fall into their laps? Their names pop up whenever people think

about certain issues or problems. They even get calls from complete strangers, out of the blue, because a mutual acquaintance recommended them. In effect, they're successful because other people think about them.

These people have mastered the art of occupying headspace.* And like almost everything else we've talked about in this book, the skills required to achieve this "miracle" are a lot easier to acquire than it might seem at first.

The key is to engage with your clients just often enough that they think of you from time to time. If you've discovered and reinforced a shared interest or a shared community with them, they might think of you as they read their hang-gliding magazines, approach that tricky sixteenth hole on the golf course you chatted about, or think about where to send their kids to college. Because you sent them a useful article on leadership a few months ago, they might think about you the next time they address an issue with a problem employee. Because you remembered they were curious about Australian rules football and sent them a note about an upcoming TV special on it, they'll think of you as a source of information. If you've simply remembered their birthday or congratulated them on the anniversary of the day they started their business (which takes no more effort than recording it in your reminder calendar), you're no longer a stranger—even if a year has gone by since your last contact.

Occupying headspace isn't complicated. It's just an expression of thoughtfulness. When you do something to occupy a small piece of someone else's headspace, the message you're sending is that they occupy a piece of yours.

The dividends can be enormous. Not only can you make a friend in the process, but occupying a client's headspace means there's a good chance they'll call you when they need information or advice or a product or service you offer.

The easiest way to start occupying headspace is to create touch points. We've already discussed creating a touch point action plan in the last chapter, but the concept deserves repeating here, because, surprisingly, a touch

*Thanks to Allan Edelson for the headspace concept.

point action plan can help you develop a long-term relationship with your client *even if your meeting didn't go as well as you had hoped.*

Remember Steve's meeting with Ian in chapter 5? Steve never crossed the credibility threshold with Ian. He didn't really answer Ian's key questions. And he talked too much. It wasn't a meeting to write home about, that's for sure. But because they'd had a prior relationship, Ian left the door open, at least a crack, for further contact. And because he still wanted to qualify for Ian's business, Steve decided he wanted to stay on Ian's radar, if possible. To do that he created a touch point action plan. Here's what it looked like:

- **Today:** Send Ian a thank-you e-mail, and be curious. Say, "In our meeting you mentioned scale a few times, and frankly I was so excited about telling you about us that I missed how important that was to you. I'm curious to know what's behind your concern."
- **Next week:** Ask my analyst to find out who supplies components to Ian's firm. See if there's a possible connection there and follow through if appropriate.
- **Start March 1:** Monthly check-ins to find out when Ian plans to be in northern California, to offer an invite for him to visit our production facility. See if my cousin can take us to the Olympic Golf Club in San Francisco to play a round.
- **Mid-March:** Given that Ian mentioned expansion, perhaps he's interested in an equity partner. Offer to put him in touch with Caroline Swallow.
- **May:** Send a box of orange golf balls when the season begins.
- **Mid-June:** Invite him for a round of golf at Brad's club (with Brad). Only good can come from them getting to know each other.
- **August:** E-mail him after first day of Masters tournament. Ask if he's interested in joining our tournament pool.
- **September:** Ask Ian if he'd like a followup meeting with Brad. Maybe a tour of their assembly plant?

If Steve follows through on each of these ideas, two things will happen: he'll stay in Ian's headspace, and he'll learn more. The more he's in Ian's headspace and the more he knows about Ian, the easier it will be to find more touch points, both in business and in their personal lives. It's a virtuous cycle.

Your touch point plans will be unique to you and your client. Some plans will have more focus on business, others on a personal connection. But each plan will stem from a genuine desire for a productive relationship.

By developing a Productive Selling attitude and practicing the skills we've presented in this book, you can become the kind of person others think about—and recommend. Over time, you will be able to occupy headspace in so many people that your phone will never stop ringing. That's an ideal outcome, especially for those of us who are accidental (and sometimes reluctant) salespeople.

Here's one thing we know for sure: the better you get at Productive Selling, the less time you'll spend *selling,* and the more time you'll devote to doing what we all naturally want to do—help people solve problems and seize opportunities.

We wish you the best success.

ACKNOWLEDGMENTS

Books are written by individuals (or sometimes, as in our case, pairs of individuals), but they are rarely the product of a single mind (or even two). It would take volumes to acknowledge everyone who influenced us in writing *Never Be Closing*. Even though we don't have space to thank you individually, you will know who you are—and how grateful we are.

There are several people, however, who deserve special mention. Without them, *Never Be Closing* would not have been written.

First, we thank Sid Parnes, to whom this book is dedicated. Sid was a remarkable, wise, and compassionate man. As a founder of the Creative Education Foundation, he taught us how to think more productively and more creatively. Sid was one of the world's great "accidental" salesmen. He persuaded thousands of people that anyone, whatever their starting point, can learn to think better.

We are indebted to the teachings and examples of professional salespeople. We thank Tom Stoyan, whose "Selling with Integrity" philosophy is deeply embedded in *Never Be Closing,* and Jacques Atz, an encyclopedia sales manager, whose take-no-prisoners strategy is not.

There are clients and friends whose imprint on our work is indelible. We thank David Olney, Kevin Mignogna, and Ken Wall. What we learned from your actions and insights has made *Never Be Closing* more useful.

We are deeply grateful to our friend and colleague Gregg Fraley for his thoughtfulness, his humor, his integrity, his creative mind, and his attitude of abundance. Without his kindness and generosity this book would not be.

No acknowledgment would be complete without thanking our literary agent, Cathy Hemming, for her tireless work on our behalf, our editor, Emily Angell, whose astute comments improved our work enormously, and our publisher, Adrian Zackheim, who had faith that *Never Be Closing* would benefit not only people who sell but people who buy.

Finally, *Never Be Closing* could not have been written without the support and forbearance of Franca Leeson (Tim's partner) and Maggie Dugan (Tim's partner) and the patience of our children, in alphabetical rather than chronological order, Branwen, Emily, Max, Molly, Peter, and Ruby.

APPENDIX: PRODUCTIVE SELLING—A REVIEW

Try to leave out the parts that readers tend to skip.

—Elmore Leonard

The following pages contain a top-line summary of the chapters of *Never Be Closing*, an outline of the Productive Selling process, and templates for its key tools.

Chapter 1 introduces the problem of the stranger's dilemma—the fact that when people who don't know each other attempt to do business, they have to overcome an initial trust barrier. Productive Selling offers a philosophy, skill set, and range of tools designed to help overcome the stranger's dilemma. It's based on a well-researched process for identifying and solving problems, and its purpose is to help you access and apply your creativity to the challenge of establishing and maintaining relationships that will be useful to you and your clients over time.

Chapter 2 introduces Productive Thinking, a framework used by a wide range of businesses and business schools to train people in creative problem solving. The six steps of the Productive Thinking model parallel the processes used by the most successful salespeople:

- Explore the current situation, identify the discomforts that need to be resolved, and establish a vision for the future.

- Define clear and measurable criteria for success in order to assess the potential effectiveness of proposed solutions.
- Articulate the questions that need to be answered to resolve the discomfort.
- Generate many creative ideas for answering those questions.
- Refine the most promising answers into robust solutions.
- Identify and recruit the resources required to create and execute a plan of action.

There are five underlying principles of Productive Thinking that apply to both innovation and effective selling:

- Avoid falling back on ingrained patterns of thinking that may no longer be useful.
- Separate creative and critical thinking; in other words, generate a long list of ideas before evaluating each individual one.
- Go beyond the first "right" answer, and instead strive for multiple "right" answers so you can choose the most promising ones.
- Be open to unexpected connections, those insights that change the way we see our issues, problems, and potentials.
- Use a deliberate debriefing process to learn from each experience and develop higher levels of skill and performance.

Chapter 3 proposes that the Productive Selling approach is useful not only for professional salespeople but also for the many people who don't think of themselves as being in sales but who are actually selling every day—whether they are employees, small business owners, entrepreneurs, or simply members of a community. Anytime someone tries to persuade someone else of the value of an idea, Productive Selling can help them do it better.

Chapter 4 discusses ethics in selling. It suggests that setting one's personal moral compass is central to both business and personal satisfaction. The Productive Selling philosophy offers a platform on which to build your own sales process that allows you to be true to yourself, to your clients, to your colleagues, and to your community. Productive Selling is a way to sell with integrity.

Chapter 5 introduces Steve, a novice salesperson who has what he thinks is a promising sales meeting with an old colleague. As it turns out, however, his colleague has a very different view of the meeting and sends Steve a "thanks, but no thanks" e-mail. Perplexed, Steve discusses his meeting with two business acquaintances, each of whom gives him different advice. Matt, a seasoned salesman, recommends concentrating on the "people" side of sales while Jane, a business school friend, suggests brushing up on process.

Chapter 6 introduces Steve's mentor, Virgil, who guides him through a simple debrief of his unsuccessful meeting and offers to teach him a sales process based on an innovation model called Productive Thinking. The remaining chapters unpack the Productive Selling model.

Chapter 7 outlines a way to design, write, and rehearse scripts that express clearly and briefly who you are, what you offer, and how you might be of value to prospective clients. Scripts can be used throughout a sales meeting and in many other situations: on the phone, in restaurants, at conferences. Effective scripts help establish your credibility, not only in terms of who you are and what you know but also in terms of how professionally you conduct yourself. Scripts can communicate the following:

- Interesting or unique things about you
- Your professional background
- Your team
- Your firm and its philosophy
- Your personal business philosophy
- Industry news and insights
- Your products and services
- Developments in your firm
- People you or your firm have helped in the past

Scripts should:

- Be brief—less than sixty seconds in length.
- Focus on one key point illustrating something unique or interesting about you or your company.
- Tell a story that includes not only facts but people.
- Be relevant to your client—some scripts will be general, others should relate directly to your prospect's industry, interests, and needs.
- Always end with a question.

Chapter 8 discusses what to do and what not to do when requesting a meeting. It proposes a five-step process:

- Find a connection, either business or personal, that will make it easy for your prospective client to say yes to your request to meet.
- Select and rehearse one or two short, relevant, topical scripts that say something intriguing about you and your company.
- Have your calendar handy so you can quickly pinpoint available times for meeting.
- Have a notepad handy so you can jot down important information.
- Always have something useful to say before making the call.

Chapter 9 presents ways to make client research efficient and productive. Your research has three objectives:

- Enhances your credibility and professionalism. The more you know about your prospect, the more effective you can be in your meeting.
- Helps you design the five areas of questioning you want to explore in your face-to-face meeting—your exploration agenda. Planning five areas of exploration gives you a fallback if one or two areas run dry.
- Helps you develop or validate ideas for delivering value to your client.

This chapter outlines where and how to find information on your prospect's core products or services; their markets, competitors, and strategic alliances; where they operate; where they manufacture; how profitable they are; how many employees they have; their market capitalization; their relationship to your market and to your competitors; and what history they have, if any, dealing with your company.

Finally, this chapter presents a powerful, time-saving research tool, Know Wonder, that can help you understand your client's situation and reveal a wealth of relevant areas to explore, both before and during your meeting.

Know	**Wonder**
List all the things you already know about your prospective client.	List things you *don't* know about the client, but might be useful if you did.

Chapter 10 outlines how to establish success criteria for your meeting (and your ongoing client relationship). The simple but powerful tool to set success criteria, called DRIVE, prompts you to define:

D — Desired outcomes for the meeting and relationship with the client.

R — Risks you need to avoid (in the meeting and the relationship).

I — Investments of time, money, and other resources you are prepared to devote to the sales effort.

V — Values you will operate by as you develop the relationship.

E — Essential, observable outcomes of the meeting (and ongoing relationship) that will indicate whether or not you have been successful.

Chapter 11 presents the Q-Notes template, a way to use your meeting notes to:

- establish an exploration agenda and followup areas of questioning.
- capture and organize the ideas you want to offer at the end of the meeting.
- record your observations about the client's interests, issues, and needs.
- create a followup checklist of touch point opportunities with your client.

Q-Notes are also the basis for your content debrief, in which you ask colleagues for ideas about how to move forward with your client.

	Discovery	Delivery
During Meeting	**Agenda Quadrant** ✓ Planned Questions: Five areas identified in your research, usually information questions starting with Who, What, Where, When, Why, or How, or simply "Tell me more about . . ." ✓ Discovered Questions: New areas you discover to explore—to return to later in the meeting.	**Value Quadrant** ✓ Planned Ideas/Suggestions to help client, generated before the meeting. ✓ Discovered Ideas/Suggestions to help client that occur to you while listening to client answer questions during meeting—how your product/service can help, people they should know, resources you can help them access.
After Meeting	**Key Information** ✓ Information you may *not* want to explore during meeting but which may be useful later. ✓ Personal information that may provide an opportunity for future touch points—perhaps something you learned during informal start of meeting or other small talk.	**Followup Checklist** ✓ Almost any idea in Quad 2 or Quad 3 may offer chance for followup conversation, such as: • Client speaking at conference in two weeks • Client's junior team has upcoming championship game • Client curious about new reporting regulations government just published

Chapter 12 proposes that a sales conversation is a three-act structure:

- Act I (which may take the first 20 to 25 percent of the meeting) is where you earn the credibility to ask your client probing questions.
- Act II (which may take about half the meeting) is where you explore your client's needs by asking a series of carefully designed questions that help you to better understand both the issues and the challenges that need to be resolved.
- Act III (which may take the final 20 to 30 percent of the meeting) is where you demonstrate usefulness by offering your client insights, resources, products or services, and the basis for a continuing relationship.

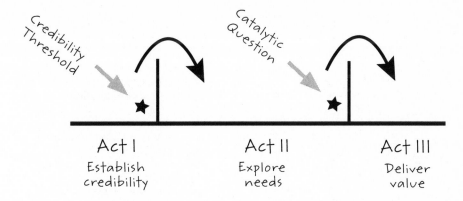

Chapter 13 describes how to recognize and communicate effectively with the six types of people you are likely to encounter in sales meetings:

- *People who are energized by* Context. These people want to fully understand a situation before jumping into it. They feel uncomfortable moving ahead too quickly.
- *People who are energized by* Results. These people focus on the facts, figures, and logic that support their goals. They value directness and efficiency.
- *People who are energized by* Ideas. These people favor abstract thinking. They enjoy proposing lots of new ideas and possible solutions to problems.
- *People who are energized by* Process. These people are systems thinkers. They want to understand how things work—and that proposed solutions will work.
- *People who are energized by* Action. These people are doers. They are persistent, decisive, and assertive. They want to see things happen.
- *People who are energized by* People. They see the world through a social lens. In evaluating proposals, their first concern is how people might be affected.

Chapter 14 describes how to leverage the time you spend in the reception area of your prospect's office, the time it takes to walk from reception to your meeting location, and the first few moments of your meeting.

The reception area is often filled with clues about the company you are visiting and the person you will meet. By becoming a Waiting Room

Jedi—exercising your curiosity, introducing yourself to the receptionist, initiating interaction with people you encounter—you can gather data that can enhance your chances of a productive meeting.

On the walk to your prospect's office, you can take advantage of the natural small talk that occurs before any meeting to discover common ground with your client—areas of shared interest, people or places that may create loose shared connections, or, if you are lucky, the possibility of a shared community. Whatever common ground you discover will contribute to a more productive conversation. To discover common ground, develop the habits of

- disclosing information about yourself and asking about your clients.
- starting right away—as soon as you say hello.
- tuning in to the clues in your client's environment.

Chapter 15 describes Act I of the sales conversation, where you earn the credibility to ask the probing questions that will be the core of the next act. There are many paths to crossing the credibility threshold. The path you choose will vary depending on the formality of the meeting, the thinking preferences of your client, the relative social status of you and your client, and the level of your sales experience. There are eight proven approaches for earning credibility that can be used independently or in combination, depending on the circumstances of your meeting:

- Strong referrals from credible sources
- Personal connections
- Business connections
- Scripts demonstrating experience and professionalism
- Process control of the meeting demonstrating competence and confidence
- Cogent industry commentary demonstrating insight
- Your reputation within the industry or wider community
- A gorilla question that assumes your credibility

As soon as you cross the credibility threshold, move immediately to the next act of the meeting, exploring your client's situation, challenges, and needs.

Chapter 16 describes Act II of the sales conversation, where the focus shifts to asking clients probing questions about their situations, challenges, and needs. Your exploration agenda for Act II is based on the five areas of questioning you've already determined from your research and noted in your Q-Notes. In Act II, remember to stay in the question; in other words, to resist the temptation to offer the prospective client ideas for solutions. It's far more productive to ask, consider, think, incubate, and record your ideas in your Q-Notes. Your purpose is to learn enough to enable you to ask one or more catalytic questions at the end of Act II, which will launch the meeting into its next act.

This chapter offers three tools to assist in your exploration: High Five, Open-Ended Questions, and AIM.

High Five is a series of five exploratory questions.

- What are your client's Itches—things that bug them, are out of balance, or create worry?
- What is the Impact of each Itch—why is it a problem?
- What Information is known (or would be useful to know) about the Itch—its causes, consequences, implications—what is not known and might be important to discover?
- Who's Involved—who's affected by the Itch, who might benefit if things were to change?
- How does the Itch link to the visions or values of the organization or its people?

You can remember the High Five questions by picturing a hand. Each finger represents a question about a word beginning with the letter *I,* and the space between the thumb and forefinger represents a question about a word beginning with the letter *V.*

Open-ended questions are invitations to think, speculate, and discuss. They cannot be answered with a yes or no (or a number or a piece of historical data). The most useful open-ended questions usually take the form of "How might we . . . ?" or "How else might we . . . ?"

AIM is an efficient way to reveal why your clients need to solve their problems, what the barriers to solution are, and what other benefits might occur if

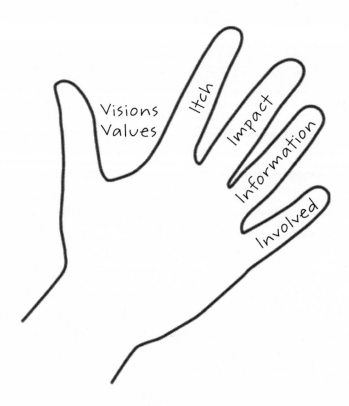

their problems were solved. AIM is an acronym that stands for Advantages, Impediments, and Maybes.

By the end of Act II, you should have gathered enough information to ask one or more catalytic questions. By design, these are usually questions without answers. They are always open ended and always look to the future. Catalytic questions often take the form of "How might . . . ?" or "How else might . . . ?" They are designed to provoke interest, clear away the fog, open the door to novel solutions, and motivate a desire to act. They are the launchpad for the ideas you will offer in the final act.

Chapter 17 suggests taking a short break from the sales meeting. Though not always possible or appropriate, an Interlude can give both you and your client a chance to incubate and reflect prior to moving into Act III. There are three effective ways to take a short break:

- Ask for a tour of your client's workspace.
- Ask to use the facilities.
- Make a personal analogy that pulls you briefly out of the business head-space of your meeting and into personal territory.

Chapter 18 describes Act III of the sales conversation, where you deliver value to your client by offering USE and making promises. USE is an acronym for Understanding, Sourcing, and Exchanging.

- You offer Understanding by providing novel perspectives and insights about your client's issues.
- You offer Sourcing by referring your client to third-party goods or services.
- You offer Exchanging by initiating a transaction for your own products, services, and ideas for resolving your client's needs.

The outcome of Sourcing and Engaging is a series of promises that propel your relationship into the future, such as:

- "I'll customize those agreements and get them to you in the morning."
- "As soon as I get back to the office, I'll send an e-mail introducing you and Harry."
- "Here are the three areas we'll focus on in the presentation."

Chapter 19 introduces three postmeeting activities that are an essential part of Productive Selling:

- The process debrief, where you identify areas for improving your performance
- The content debrief, where you mine the meeting for followup actions
- The action plan, where you begin to develop a client relationship

Chapter 20 outlines a procedure for debriefing the process of your meeting; in other words, how you handled the meeting. The process debrief answers three questions:

- What? (What happened during the meeting?)
- So What? (What did it mean?)
- Now What? (What will you do next?)

Answer the first question (What?) with Story Mapping. Using a combination of your Q-Notes and a simple timeline, tell yourself the story of the meeting, recapping as accurately as you can what happened: what you did, what you said, and what you asked—as well as what your client did, said, and asked.

Answer the second question (So What?) with the POWER tool.

POSITIVES	**E**NHANCEMENTS
What was positive or useful about the way you managed the meeting? What did you do that moved the meeting toward success? What were your strengths? Where did you shine?	How might you enhance all the Positives you listed above? How might you make your performance even stronger, even more likely to succeed?
OBJECTIONS	**R**EMEDIES
What was problematic about the way you managed the meeting? What did you do that moved the meeting away from success? What were your weaknesses? Where did you stumble?	How might you overcome the Objections you listed? How might you eliminate or reduce your weaknesses and give yourself and your process a greater chance to succeed?

WHAT ELSE?
What Else occurs to you about the way you ran the meeting? About its ups and downs? Its pacing? The way you asked questions? The way you answered them? What else about how you bridged between thoughts? About how you catalyzed? How you analogized? What else about how you began the meeting? How you brought it to a close? About your small talk? What else about the unexpected occurrences during the meeting, both welcome and unwelcome, and how you handled them? What else about yourself, about your process, about your emotions?

Answer the third question (Now What?) with the Start-Stop-Improve tool. Ask yourself: What should I stop doing? What should I start doing? What can I improve or do better?

Chapter 21 describes how to mine the meeting for followup ideas and activities. This is a three-step process:

- Prepare for the debrief by preparing a clean, legible copy of your Q-Notes.

Questions to ask	Ideas to communicate
Ask your team if there are other areas or angles you should be curious about. What are the unanswered questions? List any new questions or areas that come to mind.	Ask your team if there are any additional USE ideas that might offer value to your client. List additional information that might be useful to offer the client.
Key information (personal/business) Ask your team to capture on sticky notes any additional information they think might be useful. Invite them to list questions they think you could have asked, or could still ask, your client.	**Reasons to follow up** Ask your team to generate additional ideas for following up with the client, whether business or personal. Remind them that one good personal touch point may do more to build a relationship than ten business ones.

- Invite colleagues to a Salestorm meeting in which you review your Q-Notes and ask your team for suggestions for followup activities.
- Design a followup plan: when and how you will fulfill the promises you made, and a detailed schedule of touch points and followup activities, including who will do what by when.

Chapter 22 emphasizes the importance of following through and building on your touch point plan to maximize your chances of occupying your client's headspace, so that they think of you as a useful resource whenever they have a need.

INDEX